Indian Folklore

Indian Folklore

NOT ALL MUSLIM PEOPLE ARE TERRORISTS

Majid Hussain Nasiruddin

ISBN-13: 9781540460820
ISBN-10: 1540460827

Bismi-llāhi r-raḥmāni r-raḥīm

In the name of Allah, most gracious, most merciful.

Foreword

I am the Author of this book, I wish to express to my readers that English is not my first language. I studied in a Non-English medium school where my primary language was "Urdu" Indian language. English has been acquired language for me. Hence if there are mistakes in my book English grammar or otherwise. I wish to apologize beforehand.

Please bear with me and I hope you enjoy reading my book.

Thank you, sincerely;
Majid.H.Nasiruddin.

Introduction

My book titled, "Indian Folklore."

"Not all Muslim are terrorists."

This book has centuries old Indian folklore stories which are passed on from one generation to next generation in most educated Indian families. These are told to children age range from 12 years to 18 years by their parents. Each story has its own twist and turn and they end with a strong moral lesson. This is done to instill a very strong understanding of what is correct and what is incorrect. Hence help these children grow up to be good responsible adults.

Sub title of my story book is "Not all Muslim are terrorists." Because I am Muslim by birth and I have read the Quran with English translation. I wish to convey a message to ISIS, extremist Islamic people who feel the need to impose Sharia Law on non-Muslim people in non-Islamic countries.

CHAPTER 1

Heart Attack!

THE CANDLE BURNS BRIGHTER BEFORE IT GOES OUT. The ambulance wailed down a crowded street in Mumbai, India, the medic frantically wrestling with a crazy man strapped to a stretcher. The fifty-two-year-old Indian ripped out the drip attached to his arm. "What are you doing?" he screamed.

"Calm down," said the medic. "You had yet another massive heart attack. I'm starting an I-V line on the way to the intensive care unit.

The man screamed at the searing pain. He felt a pinch in his arm as the needle penetrated his skin, the medic administering fluids and pain meds, the shrieking ambulance dodging through crowded streets to finally pull up at the hospital's ambulance door. Face distorted with pain, Nasiruddin looked at his loving son Majid who was sitting by his side in the ambulance.

His father's voice startled Majid. "Son, we are Muslims and follow Islam. In case I become unconscious, please do not allow any doctor to put a pig's vein into my heart. We are not ever to touch the unholy animal."

Majid looked directly into his father's hopeful eyes and spoke carefully, "Abbu Ji, I hope you don't faint, but in case you do, I will make sure I tell the operating doctor about your wish against the treatment."

Nasiruddin leaned back on the stretcher, ready to surrender to death. The ambulance reached Cooper hospital in less than thirty minutes, and Majid could see his father being rushed to the operation theater.

Majid had witnessed his father going in and out of ICU many times, yet this time his dad looked very anxious. Majid hurried along with his father toward ICU.

Doctor Kulkarni, who had treated Nasiruddin many times, stopped Majid at the door. "Patients only! No relatives allowed inside ICU."

Hurriedly Majid explained, "As per my dad's wishes, he does not want to have a pig's vein put into his blocked arteries."

Doctor Kulkarni shook his head. "I know your father. I have treated him here many times. I'm aware of his stubborn wish not to use a pig's vein in his heart. Now if you will excuse me, I have to attend to him at once. Please wait outside in the lobby area. I will let you know when your dad is out of danger."

Majid walked back to the lobby, sat down, and closed his eyes. He remembered the many times his father had lain in a bed in the hospital. Now he'd suffered a fifth heart attack. Majid believed these heart attacks were caused by twenty-year battle to retrieve his rights to the eighty acres of land stolen by his greedy uncles. Stress caused the first heart attack summer of 1982. Plaque blocked the arteries, and his doctors wanted to treat the angina with open heart surgery. The blocked artery would be replaced with a vein or biological tissue from a pig. His father, being a Muslim, refused the treatment option explaining, "In my religion, pigs are unholy animals. Muslims are not even allowed to touch these unclean animal. I will not permit any pig's part to go in my heart."

The frustrated surgeon replied, "Then, Nasiruddin, your days are numbered. Your next heart attack could be your last."

Nasiruddin was given medications to thin his blood. Even with the threat of another heart attack, he had made every attempt to get his land back from his greedy uncles, and continued to challenge the corrupt court and judges. Nasiruddin had taken the matter to the New Delhi supreme court. He fought hard from 1982 until 1987.

Upon hearing Dr. Kulkarni's voice Majid, who had been dozing in a chair outside the ICU, opened his eyes.

"Hello, young man. Your father is out of danger for now, but we are keeping him over the weekend to monitor his heart and overall health. If you wish, you may visit him now. He is being moved to bed number 17, fourth room to your left."

Majid walked into private ICU room number 17 to see his father lying in bed with IV lines in his left hand, and a heart monitor attached to his chest. A screen displayed his heart rhythm which the doctor said appeared stable.

The young man spoke to his father. "Abbu Ji, your condition seems stable now, but Doctor Kulkarni has decided to keep you under observation over the weekend. He assures me he'll let you go Monday morning if your condition remains stable. I'm going home to eat, and will bring lunch for you. You're supposed to have light food and lots of fluids for next 24 hours or so."

Nasiruddin described what he'd like to eat. "My son, have your mother make me khichdi easy and simple rice lentil dish made healthy, nutritious and delicious just under 30 minutes, and foods that are nutritious yet easy to digest. Oh, and bring me some coconut juice."

"Yes, Abbu Ji, I will eat my lunch at home and bring your food as soon as mom is done cooking it. I'll see you shortly."

On the way out Majid paused in front of the doctor. "Thank you very much, doctor Kulkarni."

Two hours later Majid returned with food, a straw, and a fresh coconut. This healthy diet continued throughout the weekend.

Majid reminisced. Today is July 31st, 1987. My father felt severe pain in his heart again and was admitted to the emergency ward. It's his third night at the hospital. He's recovering fairly well, but he's still begging me to bring him a pack of cigarettes. I'm only seventeen. Even though he's my father, I must disobey his request.

And so Majid answered dad, "Abbu Ji, this is a non-smoking hospital. Even if I bring you a cigarette, which I won't, where will you smoke it?"

His father rationalized, "The IV line is on a stand with wheels. I'll take it to the balcony at night and have a smoke. I need a cigarette and some fresh air."

Majid pleaded with his father, "Abbu Ji, don't you wish to see me grow up? The doctor already said your next cigarette could be your last. Your heart needs oxygen and smoking will kill you, so I will not bring you cigarettes."

His father sighed, knowing his young son was right. Instead, the old man pleaded, "Will you stay with me a little bit longer today? I feel like talking to you.

"Son, I asked Doctor Kulkarni this morning when I'll be allowed to go home. He wishes me to stay over today and tonight, but promised I can go home tomorrow, Saturday morning. After I get discharged from this hospital, I'll quit smoking and get up early in the morning to watch you play soccer. Then we can take long walks together on Juhu Beach. We'll drink fresh coconut water together then come home and play chess until lunch time. Oh, I have so much to show you. We shall go to Delhi where we can pray together at the Jama mosque.

"Yes, Abbu Ji. We shall do all that. But first, get well."

CHAPTER 2

"Have Brain and no money."

Majid's father clutched Majid's hand. "I have so much to tell you, to teach you, son. Do what you love for work. That love will help you get better at it. The money will become the by-product of your love for your job."

"I know. You have told me that many times. It is late. Get some sleep."

His father wouldn't let go of Majid's hand. His eyes lit up. "Let me first tell you a story."

Majid loved his father's stories, often taken from Indian folk lore tales. They had a twist and a moral.

"Only one story."

"There is more than one story son but my heart feels like telling you these stories please bear with me and listen to them."

Nasiruddin says, "Son, this first story is about having a good brain but no money."

Sixteenth century India was considered a golden bird with many kings with their own kingdoms, among such a kingdom in northern part of India, lived a very wise wealthy king named, Aurangzeb Mogul, with his wise noble advisor always by his side name, Alamgir Hikmat.

Once a month king Aurangzeb liked going through his entire kingdom with his wife, a 11 years old son and his trusted noble advisor Alamgir to see how people of his kingdom are doing, this was also a chance for many people to see their king and have an open opportunity to talk to their king directly without any fears, hesitation or restrictions from any one.

While the king was passing through the crowded Bazar Street, he could not help but notice a sign written in bold letters:

"I have brain but no money."

A decently dressed man holding that sign stood by the sidewalk.

The king asked Alamgir, his wise advisor who was mostly with him, "What is the matter with this man, standing there holding this unusual sign?"

Alamgir exclaimed, "King Aurangzeb, that person is mentally ill and does little work. People don't know much about him as he does not talk much with anyone. I would recommend you ignore him. Let's keep moving on."

But the king was simply too curious about this man and wanted to talk to him there and then.

Alamgir advised the king that since everyone is convinced he was mad it was not safe to speak to him. Call him to your palace where you are more securely guarded. There the madman can explain himself and the sign that he is holding.

The next day morning the madman appeared in King Aurangzeb's palace and was watched very carefully by all of the king's men. The king asked the man his name.

The nut seemed very educated in a way he replied to the king, "Your honor, esteem king Aurangzeb, your humble servant is known by many names by many people, my late parents named me Azimuddin. If you wish to address me as Azim, I would be most pleased with it."

King was half way sold to this man already, and asked his next question, "Azim, why don't you work like other men do? and why do you rather stand with a sign which says "I have brain but no money," Could you explain yourself to me?"

Azim said, "As you must have already known about me, I do not talk much with anyone unless I see a gain or a reason for conversation."

"I was asked to come here because you showed interest in meeting me."

And honestly, "I was almost dragged here much against my wishes, now you want to know why I stand at Bazar street with a sign?"

By explaining myself, "What would I gain king Aurangzeb?, Do you think it's fair for you to pick up anyone that draws your attention, and interest and get them to explain themselves to you because you just happen to be a king?"

Aurangzeb was sitting with his wife and 11-year- old son next to him with other prominent men of King, friends, and advisors.

At this point, Aurangzeb's soldiers were looking for a sign from their king for arresting this man who had the courage to talk to their king in this manner.

Aurangzeb admired the man's courage and his bluntness, in the manner in which he spoke.

King apologized to Azim and said, "What it would take for you to explain yourself to me?"

Azim simply spoke very calmly and said, "I will need Rs.1000.00 to share details of my signage "Have brain but no money." that I hold on the Bazar street and a year to prove my wisdom to anyone who doubts my abilities."

King decided to grant Rs.1000 to the Azim after handing him the money king said, "Now you may explain yourself to me."

Azim being blunt as he was, only said, "Do you pay attention to what I say and how I say it?"

King's advisor Alamgir, started walking towards Azim, pulling his sword out.

King Aurangzeb held his hand out signaling Alamgir to hang on, and asked Azim again, "Didn't you say, you would speak when you see a gain in it for you, now that I have given you Rs.1000.00 why would you not tell me the reason for that sign?"

Azim replied to Aurangzeb, "I also mentioned it will take me one year to prove my wisdom to anyone who doubts me."

"And my wisdom is a part of the signage that I hold so bravely."

" You could either wait for a year and guaranteed you will gain ten times more than Rs.1000.00, or you can simply have your Rs.1000.00 back now and kindly allow me to walk away free, as I was before I came here this morning."

So King Aurangzeb spoke, this time, a bit harshly, "Azim, by far it has been an exciting morning for me."

"I am thrilled to meet a man, who is so courageous, blunt, and confident of himself."

"Yet he is asking to walk away with my Rs.1000.00 offering me not much choice."

"Than to wait a year to get the answer that I rather have this moment."

"Mr. Azim, I am aware that you do not have much to offer materialistically to anyone, and yet you claim that you will pay me back ten times more for this Rs.1000.00 using your wisdom in a matter of one year."

Taking a pause to have a sip of water, then king Aurangzeb said to Azim almost as in Lions roar, "Azim, I Aurangzeb Mogul, state this in front of my entire advisors, friends, my family, soldiers."

"That exactly after a year from today, if I do not receive my Rs.1000.00 back."

"I will behead you, cut off your head in front of my entire kingdom, do you agree with me Mr. Azim?"

"Or do you wish to return my Rs.1000.00 back and let's consider this morning never happened, and I shall allow you to walk free from here, and you can have my word on it."

Azim noticed the all of the king's friends, advisors and soldier's eyes were at him.

Azim spoke again, as calmly as the morning breeze, "Respected king Aurangzeb, as I had said, I do not talk much, but when I do talk, I always know what I am talking about."

"And I only say what I can do, and in most cases my actions speak louder than words."

" Your trusted spies could not do much homework on me otherwise, they would have found out and would have known."

"That I am a defeated king of Greece myself, I lost my war against Romanians and fled with my life took a merchant's ship that sailed towards India."

"But that does not mean I am not a wise man; this is why I am unable to toil as other men do because I don't know how."

"Enough being said about me, King Aurangzeb."

" I will see you after a year with Rs.1000.00 or more Rupees, in the mean time I would request absolutely no interference from your men for next one year in whatever I choose to do with your money or how I spend my next year, what so ever."

Aurangzeb agreed to the terms, and Azim simply wished the King had a good day and walked in the same calm manner out as he had walked in.

Upon Alamgir's advise King Aurangzeb agreed, that Azim, be kept an eye on carefully, and daily and weekly reports on Azim, be submitted to King Aurangzeb, by kings trusted spies and also find out as quickly as possible if Azim is indeed a defeated king of Greece. For sure King Aurangzeb's detectives figured out as Azim had said he was a king of Greece up until six months ago. Aurangzeb felt that piece of information was calming. The first report from his spies explained that Azim is enjoying the Rs.1000.00 of Aurangzeb. He had invited the entire village for a hearty dinner and improved his living conditions and employed almost 100 young men and gave them wages that even King Aurangzeb would think twice about.

Days turn into weeks and weeks into months, and Azim is only living as if he is on a long luxurious vacation, Alamgir wanted to go and inquire what Azim was up to, but Aurangzeb requested that he be left alone.

Almost after the third month, Azim had his men collect cow dunk in a great quantity to a point where storing this entire cow dunk required a separate field which Azim arranged. By the end of the fourth month, all of this cow dunk was made into flatbread shape called Uppli, in India. These Uppli's were laid in the second significant ground, under hot scorching sun to dry, while one set of Uppli get sun baked, next is ready and all of which is stored in a third largest ground. King Aurangzeb's spies were very puzzled along with Alamgir and king Aurangzeb himself, everybody was eager to know what is Azim up to, but they were told to leave Azim alone for one year. In the third ground, Azim decided to burn this entire flat shaped cow dunk which was burned in small portions, for day and nights, and the ash that was collected after burning cow dunk, which was stored in cloth sacks which were no larger than regular grain sacks.

Alamgir was very upset at this point said to Aurangzeb, "Till this moment we could have made a little bit money from the shaped cow dunk, but Azim burned it all, it's like he is burning your money away."

Aurangzeb, who lacked patience, somehow managed to keep his calm and said to Alamgir, "I will be only very pleased to cut off Azim's head if he does not produce my Rs.1000.00 back after a year is done."

Monsoon season was soon to start, where it rains in India from June to the end of September. Azim had his working men take all of the burnt cow dunk sacks to the shore of long deserted beaches.

And laid them down barely within few feet of high tide waters of the sea, because of a vast number of sacks there was almost a small wall of bags, for many miles along the shore of the entire beach. And after the last of the sacks were laid on beaches, Azim thanked all men for their hard work and asked them to take few months off. People enjoyed working for Azim as he was paying them handsomely and didn't make them work as much.

The leader of the working group said to Azim, "We will all be available if you require any further services from us."

Azim thanked the manager and said, "I will let you know if you and your men's services are needed again."

It was the eleventh month of the contract, and King Aurangzeb's spy's almost had nothing to say about their daily weekly reports other than how Azim, is enjoying delicious lunches and dinners with various friends who travel from far places to meet with Azim.

Aurangzeb could not bear it anymore. So one morning he sent his soldiers with Alamgir to bring Azim to his Palace, upon arrival.

Azim inquired, "What is the urgency as there is still one more month left of that 'one year' contract?"

Aurangzeb was not in the mood, for any further smooth talking, Aurangzeb said, "I demand that my Rs.1000.00 be produced at once, or I will behead you, cut off your head before the afternoon in front of my entire kingdom."

Seeing the urgency of the situation, Azim spoke to the king, "I have given time off to all of my employees to return only last week of this month; hence, I am required to use your soldiers to bring those sacks from the beach over here to your palace at once."

King Aurangzeb ordered some of his soldiers to go to the beach in horse driven carriage and pick up ten sacks to begin with and bring it back.

Once soldiers reach the beach, soldiers could not lift up the sacks single-handedly.

As they seemed to weigh a lot, it took two or three soldiers to pick each and every sack carefully and loaded it in their carriage.

Soldiers were wondering it is only wet ash from cow dunk why would it be so heavy? But they dared not open the sack and brought the sacks back to the palace.

Azim requested those sacks be opened, and the first sack that was opened had Oyster's in it along with many Mussels and Clams. The very first oyster Azim opened had a large Pearl in it and so the next one and one after.

Aurangzeb could barely believe his eyes, and got soldiers to start opening remaining of the sacks and within an hour, fifty soldiers were working on finding Pearls of various shapes sizes and color.

And Azim said to King Aurangzeb, "Just within these sacks you have more pearls than the Rs.1000.00 I owed you, and there are many more sacks at the beach which will also have Pearls in them. Now if you are done with me, I have lunch arrangements to be kept with some of my dear friends."

And Azim was headed towards the door.

Aurangzeb asked, "Azim please stop and have a quick talk with me."

And Azim came closer to Aurangzeb and said, "Okay, please make it a fast and a quick talk."

Aurangzeb said, "I will share half of these Pearls with you Azim provided you explain to me how did this miracle happen?"

Azim replied, "What seem like a miracle, are things working in your favor with precise timing and calculating every step of the way carefully planned."

Here is how your Miracle took place Aurangzeb, "Oysters, lives in salty sea waters and craves a drop of sweet rainwater. Usually, during the year, they depend on dew drops to collect in their mouths which do not happen often."

"But during monsoon season the rains occur at various times of the day and night, especially early in the morning sea is usually very calm which allows oysters to keep their hold steady in the sand while they keep their clams mouth open for that whole thick raindrop to fall in their mouth. Lots of birds of prey along with seagulls and cranes wait for the oysters and clams by the seashore."

"And quickly pick them up to eat, once the bird finds the food they usually like to sit at the nearest wall or lamp post or a tree."

"But since our beaches have nothing around them, but those sacks that I laid very close to the sea shore. Hence they sit on these sacks but being wet from rain and high sea tides these sacks are very fragile, and hence bird's legs start to sink in as quickly as they sit on these sacks, most birds in their panic drop these oysters and clams in these sacks and fly away."

Hence, these sacks get filled with these Pearl-bearing oysters, clams, and mussels. Had we waited another month these sacks would have been filled up even more, as last month of the monsoon gets most rains.

Aurangzeb was hearing Azim's every word carefully and asked, "Did you know of this trick from before, have you tried it in the past?"

Azim said, "His kingdom was one of the wealthiest because of his Pearl collecting skill which he had not shared with anyone till today."

Aurangzeb kept his word and gave half of collected pearls to Azim and Azim thanked King Aurangzeb and went on his merry way.

Aurangzeb asked Alamgir, "What do you think we learn from this experience Alamgir?"

Alamgir didn't know how to answer Aurangzeb, so he politely asked, "How would you describe this experience, Aurangzeb?"

Aurangzeb said, "I would only say, listen to the most foolish looking people.'

"The entire Bazar street thought Azim to be a madman and won't even care to see why he was holding the Sign?"

"Have brain, but no money", but in actuality, he indeed knew how to make the money but didn't have an investment to put his money making plans together."

"But there was something about the way he behaved, his sense of dressing."

"And the way he spoke to me at our first meeting, gave me the courage to try Azim out, and my gamble paid off well."

"So listen to fools, even they may have something a wise man can learn from, at the same time don't make assumptions about people or don't judge them till you have given them their fair chance to prove themselves, I think Alamgir this is what I have learnt from this experience."

And entire courthouse in the private chambers of the Palace stood up and clapped for their wise king Aurangzeb.

Nasiruddin said, "Son are you ready for the next one, it's about king Aurangzeb finding his wife on a hunting spree."

Majid said, "I love your stories Abbu Ji, please go ahead and tell me."

CHAPTER 3

Meeting wife on Hunting Spree

"Son, you must be wondering, how could anyone find their wife on a hunting trip?"

"Here is how son."

Many kings during this era, like to spend warm summer days going on a hunt for a buck or deer or whatever else they may find, tigers roam most forest and many kings had lost their men or their own lives to the vicious beast, hence great caution was used during hunting sprees.

On a beautiful sunny summer morning in month of May, king Aurangzeb, decided to go hunting, king Aurangzeb was out on a hunt, and while chasing a stag, having an excellent Arabian big black horse, he left most of his men behind in pursuit of a stag, stag kept running through thick forest and after almost half hour of chase Aurangzeb decided to let the stag run away and this is when he realized that his advisor Alamgir and his soldiers were nowhere to be seen, he tried to follow the direction of sunset and came upon a small village where he found a well and few people around it. He quickly reached the well upon reaching the well he could not help but notice an exceedingly beautiful looking woman, she wore simple clothes, light blue color dress, which complimented her fair skin well, she had long black straight silky hair, an oval face, sharp nose, high cheek bones and most beautiful hazel eyes king had ever seen, Aurangzeb felt as his heart is ready to jump out of his chest, Aurangzeb was very handsome himself, his height 5.11, he swam almost every day in a lake right within the walls of his own fort, Aurangzeb, had high cheek bones, sharp nose and hazel eyes himself, Aurangzeb guessed the woman's height to be 5.6 or 5.8 she was definitely a little bit shorter in height then him, she was filling up the water pot, he approached the well further and people right away noticed the handsome Aurangzeb and also noticed that he was a king by the way he was dressed, Aurangzeb requested some water which he was given and he asked the beautiful woman her name, "What is your name, you look young, very beautiful, and charming?"

She felt shy & blushed at the same time, but knowing a king is asking, she politely replied, "My name is Dilras Banu Begum."

Right away king Aurangzeb said, in soft voice, "I would be most delighted to meet your parents at once Dilras."

Dilras thought what would a handsome king want with her parents but once again knowing king is asking she willfully obliged. And Dilras started walking towards her home along a narrow path with thick shrub growing on either side of the path way, during their short walk Aurangzeb found out from talking to Dilras that she is a princess herself but like to come out to well with friends and help bring water back to her palace. Her father Mirza Safavi, and mother Nauras banu begum, have been living in their kingdom all their lives, Dilras started approaching a decent looking palace. Dilras's father right away noticed the king is following their daughter on his magnificent black horse, to their home so he ran to the door to greet the king, after the initial introduction, Mirza, eagerly asked how he can be of some service to the king. Mirza requested Aurangzeb to come in their home which he did, as he stepped in Dilras's palace, he could notice Dilras's palace was tastefully decorated with light blue color wall, nice large painting of a beautiful sunrise by the ocean was hung on the wall, the entire palace had a very welcome look to it. Aurangzeb was asked to sit down on handmade wooden sofa chair which was woven in silk and as soon as Aurangzeb sat in it reminded him of his beautiful big comfortable throne that he has been sitting in to address many matters of his kingdom, Mirza then quickly asked if he can offer something to the king to drink, Aurangzeb requested a glass of cold water. Mirza was still standing out of respect for the king, this is when Aurangzeb said to Mirza, "Have a seat Mirza, this is of course your own palace, I understand your respect for me by standing there but I wish to talk to you and would like you to sit."

Mirza felt a bit more relaxed, having a king in your home seldom happens in his small kingdom. So Aurangzeb, spoke in his usual soft kind voice by stating, "I am a sixth King of Mogul Dynasty. I rule most land of India subcontinent, I am 27 years old and since my teenage I always dreamed of a beautiful woman like your daughter to be my wife, when I saw your daughter for a moment I felt my dream just turned into reality, so this is what has brought me to your palace, so Mirza, I would like to propose your daughter's hand in marriage with me."

Mirza had a big smile on his face, because he would have never thought in his wildest dream that his little girl princess Dilras, who had grown up to be a beautiful young woman was going to be a queen of Mogul Dynasty. Dilras who was listening to this conversation from the kitchen of her home started jumping with Joy in front of her mother.

Mirza said to Aurangzeb, "I love my daughter just like any good father would. Before I give you any answer's I would like to talk to my daughter first after all it is her life we are talking about here, I just want to make sure that she has just as much say in this matter as you or me, she has the right to accept or refuse your offer to marry her."

King Aurangzeb nervously said, "Well of course, I would not like to marry a woman that does not feel the same about me as I about her."

By this time mother of Dilras came to the living room very classy looking woman elegantly dressed in her 50's and said to Mirza, and king Aurangzeb, "You see king Aurangzeb, kings don't come over to our small kingdom, you are the first king to step foot in our home so Dilras is as it is excited about having a king visit her home and she kept her ears glued to the living room to hear every word of your conversation with her father, the moment you asked for her hand in marriage, she started jumping with joy in the kitchen so the answer to your question to marry our daughter is "YES."

Following week Dilras and king Aurangzeb got married Dilras parents were amazed at looking at every details of beautiful fort inside which had many beautiful palaces with its own gardens and swimming pools and horses, within the walls of the fort were homes of people who lived in Aurangzeb's great kingdom and followed by further walls of king's palaces which were well surrounded by high strong walls with in the fort structure. So grand wedding celebration lasted for 3 days. Fireworks in the evening, king prepared a grand buffet for his whole kingdom, many of king's friends and relatives were asked to come attend the king Aurangzeb's wedding on a short notice and many friends and relatives did turn up. King Aurangzeb looked up the clear blue sky of summer of India and thanked Allah for all his blessings, I have health on my side, I am one of the wealthy king of India, I have a beautiful wife.

"Dilras likes me just as much as I like her and Aurangzeb was sure this liking in no time will turn into true unbreakable bonding of loving husband and wife as married couple."

He was already thinking of many places in this world where he would like to go for his honeymoon.

Next year king was blessed with a son, Aurangzeb named him "Mazuddin" Mazuddin was growing up very smart by each year.

So my dear son, "Majid this is how when Aurangzeb met Azim for the first time, he already had his wife and a 11 years old son sitting next to him."

"Are you enjoying these stories my son?"

It was already 10pm, Majid enjoyed the story and said to his father, "It was a very good story Abbu Ji."

So Majid's father said, "My son are you ready for the next one?"

Majid replied earnestly, "Yes Abbu Ji."

"I love these stories Abbu Ji, please tell me more."

CHAPTER 4

Five lessons worth fifty thousand Rupees

King Aurangzeb and his wife Dilraz, went on many trips together with their intelligent growing son and the entire kingdom was happy to see so much love between their king and queen. Aurangzeb was very curious by nature and paid attention to minor details in everything he did whereas Dilraz paid attention only to main points and sometimes missed the small things. Aurangzeb and Dilraz, along with Alamgir, the king's advisor, and a few soldiers, always went around their kingdom the first week of the month to address the questions and concerns of as many people as they could during a long day-trip around their entire kingdom. Many people came to greet their beloved king and queen and also looked forward to this day so they could get help from their king and queen who were very generous with their money toward everyone that lived in their kingdom. On one such trip Aurangzeb met Azim, who had given him an enormous amount of money. But it had been close to two years since Aurangzeb had heard of or seen Azim.

King Aurangzeb had just finished his monthly tour of his kingdom when his general soldier came to him, saying, "Azimuddin is back. This time he is holding a sign: 'Five Lessons Worth Fifty Thousand Rupees.' He is standing on the Bazar street again."

Aurangzeb knew how beneficial this Azim fellow had been to him last time and decided to see him right away. He thought to himself, "Even if I give fifty thousand Rupees to Azim, I will still have a lot of pearls left from his last wise trick, so basically I will be paying him back some of his own money. I have nothing to lose and everything to gain."

With this thinking he sent Alamgir to bring Azim to his private room at once. Alamgir brought Azim back to the palace in a comfortable carriage.

King Aurangzeb invited him to a hearty breakfast and they spoke as if they were good friends.

Aurangzeb said, "It's been a while. How are you, Azimuddin? What have you been doing these last two years? How come you are holding yet another sign? Have you spent all the money from your pearl deal with me two years ago?"

Right away Azim said, "I requested you call me Azim, not Azimuddin. Perhaps you forgot in the last two years. Aurangzeb, has anyone taught you to ask one question at a time? You are very curious, and since I know you to be a just king, I will answer all your questions."

Aurangzeb thought, "Oh Allah, he is still as blunt as he used to be."

Then Aurangzeb asked again, only this time he called the man Azim. Azim said he was fine. He had been traveling in faraway lands for the last two years, giving money to people who were far more in need of money than he was. When his money ran out he came back to Aurangzeb's kingdom, knowing well if anyone would buy what he had to sell, it would be Aurangzeb, who was by far the most curious king Azim had met.

Aurangzeb asked, "What are these five lessons worth fifty thousand Rupees? Please tell me Azim?"

Azim said, "May I have the money first? Ten thousand for each lesson, which needs to be implemented in practical life to fully understand and acknowledge."

Aurangzeb had Alamgir bring in five stacks with ten thousand Rupees in each stack. Aurangzeb said, "Azim, this is fifty thousand. When you tell me each lesson, you can take another stack of ten thousand. For five lessons, here are your fifty thousand Rupees."

After taking the first ten thousand, Azim said, "Lesson number one: if you wish to learn something new, you must completely lose your identity. Only then may you learn something new that you would never know, being the famous king that you are. People are bound to treat you differently, knowing very well that you are a king."

Aurangzeb asked, "How do you suggest I do that, Azim?"

Azim said, "That brings me to my second lesson, lesson number two."

Azim, the wise man took another ten thousand, and he spoke as usual, in his calm manner. "Aurangzeb, you should leave your kingdom looking like a common man, wearing very ordinary clothes and perhaps growing facial hair to further hide your identity."

Aurangzeb said, "Azim, I am a king. If I go anywhere looking like a simple person, especially outside of my kingdom, if I am recognized by any of my enemies, this could put my life at risk."

Azim was anticipating this response, so he simply replied, "In that case you may take Alamgir, your trustworthy advisor, or a trustworthy soldier, but even his identity must be kept a secret just as yours."

Aurangzeb could not wait to hear the third lesson, so he asked, "Azim, what is the third lesson?"

Azim said, "Lesson number three: you must show respect and appreciation for other people's choices. For example, this diamond studded gold bracelet you are wearing. Now, I hate gold ornaments of any kind on a man. This is my own personal taste, Aurangzeb, but if you were to ask me, 'Azim, what do you think of my Gold bracelet?,' knowing well that you must like it enough to wear it, I would look to see what is good about this Gold bracelet even though I think it looks hideous, and I would simply say, 'This Gold bracelet looks good on your wrist. I am sure it gives you pleasure wearing it.' I might even ask if this Gold bracelet has any significant value emotionally or financially. Maybe it was gifted or presented to you by your father, who passed away a few years ago, and hence its value is emotional. Or maybe you purchased this Gold bracelet from most honored goldsmith of his time, and hence it is very expensive and, again, financially valuable."

Azim asked Aurangzeb if he understood what Azim was trying to explain.

Aurangzeb said, "Look for the good even in bad things."

Azim said, "Very well said. I wish I knew how to cut long stories short like you just did, but I am what most people call long winded."

By Aurangzeb's expression Azim could tell Aurangzeb was ready to hear the fourth lesson.

"Lesson number four," said Azim. "Aurangzeb, many times in our lives, we are presented with situations that we do not know how to handle. Sometimes we accidentally learn of other people's secrets or things that would hurt someone's feelings, thus causing great emotional pain. I wonder what I should use as an example, Aurangzeb, but it is always good to use our best judgment during these trying times. Simply try to understand what could have caused that situation to occur in the first place, try to put yourself in the person's shoes, and think about all the pros and cons before you say anything or do anything. Sometimes it's better simply to leave it alone, as Allah has a way of working things out mysteriously."

Aurangzeb seemed really eager to hear the fifth lesson, so Azim continued speaking. "Lesson number five: when you are angry, no matter what has caused that anger, do not do anything in that moment. Get a glass of cold water, take more than three minutes to drink it, and wait for at least twenty-four hours before you do anything about the incident or person that caused you to feel angry. It is difficult, as you want to act on the impulse and do something about it there and then.

"Here is an example. It might not be the best example, but here is what I can think of off the top of my head. Once there was a young man known in the entire village for being very short tempered. Let's say his name was Gussa. Since he was healthy and well built, most people around him were careful not to offend him, as he might beat a person who offended him. Due to his temper no one wanted him to marry their daughters, as they were frightful that he might beat their daughters up.

"One day an old man from another village came to Gussa's village, looking to find a suitor to marry his daughter. Right away he noticed Gussa's good-built body and good looks, as Gussa was very handsome. At once he thought of giving his daughter's hand in marriage to Gussa, so he decided to talk to Gussa. While they were in conversation, the old man said something that offended Gussa, and as expected, Gussa, instantly and without a second thought, slapped the old man. When other people noticed this, they quickly came to the old man's rescue. The old man who got slapped said, 'I tried to talk to him only because I thought I had met a man who was handsome and whom my daughter could be married to, but not someone with such a short temper.' Hence Gussa spent a lonely life without many friends or a wife, so anger is not good."

Aurangzeb agreed with all five of Azim's lessons. Azim put the money in his bag, and after having a hearty dinner with Aurangzeb, he bid the king farewell. The following week, after giving it considerable thought over the weekend, Aurangzeb decided to try out the five lessons in practical life to see what he could learn from them. So he called his wife, Dilraz; his son; and his trusted friend and advisor, Alamgir, and said, "I wish to test these five lessons."

Alamgir said, "These five lessons have severe requirements to put them to the test. Are you sure you want to do this, Aurangzeb?"

Aurangzeb said, "Yes."

Dilraz said, "Dear Aurangzeb, I love you so much. I will miss you if you go away."

Aurangzeb said, "But I have to go away, and who knows how far and for how long? But know it in your heart that I love you and always will."

Alamgir decided to go with Aurangzeb. They decided to go southwest, knowing the weather was usually much better in the southwestern part of the kingdom. So Aurangzeb and Alamgir dressed up like average-looking men. They started walking as normal people do, but Alamgir insisted that they both go by horse, as they would be traveling for days and nights. After almost a month or so, Aurangzeb felt he must now be far away from his own kingdom, and the next kingdom would be a good kingdom to stay for a while and try out these five lessons. It was pitch dark, so Aurangzeb and Alamgir slept in their tents, waiting for the next morning to enter this kingdom.

It was bright in the morning, just before sunrise. Early on in their journey they had decided Alamgir would lead and Aurangzeb was to follow closely behind. Alamgir liked the idea of leading Aurangzeb by a few feet, knowing if there was any kind of danger or trouble, he would handle it before his king was threatened. So Alamgir stayed few steps ahead so that he could look out for snakes and other kinds of dangerous animals that roamed the forest.

As Alamgir passed through the gates of this kingdom, called Jhansi, everybody started shouting, "Long live our new king."

Alamgir was a bit surprised and eagerly asked what was going on. Why would they mistake Alamgir as their king? An old wise-looking man came up to Alamgir. When Aurangzeb caught up enough to listen, the wise old man said, "Our beloved king passed away yesterday evening, and he does not have any children who can rightfully take over his throne. Our king did not think that anyone in the entire kingdom of Jhansi would be able to manage his beautiful kingdom, so he made a wish before his death: the first man that walked through these gates at sunrise was to be taken as our king. So, Mister, may I know your name so I can tell all these people, who are now your servants, their king's name?"

Alamgir said he needed a quick moment to think and talk to his friend first. He spoke to Aurangzeb. "What should I do? I wish to nominate you as these people's king. What should our names be? Remember we are supposed to keep our identities hidden."

Aurangzeb said, "I am Aurang, you are Alam, and you will be their king."

Alamgir was bit hesitant, but seeing as Aurangzeb meant it, he followed his instructions. Alamgir faced the old wise man again and said, "My name is Alam, and this is my best friend, Aurang. Since I am your king now, I nominate Aurang as my advisor, to be guarded and respected just as much as your king at all times."

As Alam stepped inside the castle, he could not help but notice that this was indeed a very wealthy kingdom. Even the king's throne had rubies and diamonds embedded in it. Breakfast was already set out, and Alam insisted that Aurang be allowed to eat with him. Both Aurang and Alam were hungry and tired from their long journey, so after breakfast they rested for two hours. When they woke up, the older wise man, who was the advisor of the dead king, introduced Alam to all the generals of his army and the king's personal servants and spies. Before long Alam had been introduced to just about every important person in his new kingdom. Alam wrote down in a book the many people's names and their positions.

Both Aurang and Alam were enjoying their new lives, with hunting trips and beautiful women singing and dancing every evening, followed by excellent dinners. It seemed as though every chef in the kingdom was trying to please the new king. Alam quickly had to resume all the duties of a king, including maintaining friendly relationships with kingdoms that were as strong as his and visiting many towns and villages. Alam decided to do things as King Aurangzeb used to do them in his own kingdom, and he always kept Aurang very close to him and asked for his advice and suggestions from time to time.

One day, Alam was getting ready to go deer hunting, most kings did it as sports hunting not to eat the animal, but Aurang was feeling slightly under the weather, so he decided not to go. Alam sent for a doctor right away and even appointed a personal care attendant for Aurang. When Alam was ready to leave for his hunting trip, a trusted soldier asked to come along; he said he was good at protecting his king and knew of many places where hunting was really good. Alam agreed to take a few soldiers along. As expected, after traveling through the forest for two days, the king found himself in the thickest parts of the forest, where tigers, leopards, panthers, stags, and deer were everywhere. The king set up his hunting tent in one of the biggest, tallest trees and hunted four deer, a stag, and two tigers. Almost after a week, when food supplies started running dangerously low, the king and the soldiers decided it was time to leave. A wise soldier suggested, "There is a village not too far from where we are. Perhaps the king would like to go visit the village and purchase more food for the journey back home."

Alam liked the suggestion, and they all headed to the village. When Alam and the soldiers were hardly inside the gates of the village, Alam could not help but notice the most stunning woman he had ever laid eyes on. She must have been no more than twenty-five years of age and wore a light-orange silk dress showing her curvy body. She had long silky hair, light-brown eyes, high cheekbones, a sharp nose, and full pink lips. Alam thought she looked like a Greek goddess. He fell in love with her instantly. He had a soldier follow her to see where she lived. By afternoon the soldier came back with many details about the woman. The soldier said, "Her name is Amina Banu. She is twenty-three years old and is the daughter of a poor pot maker, she lives on the northwest side of this village, and she is single."

King Alam heard only the last part of the soldier's information: "She is single."

Alam thought to himself. I am thirty-eight years old. There is a fifteen-year age gap between us. But he reminded himself. I am no longer a mere advisor or a friend of a king. I am a king by myself. After rationalizing his thoughts, he came to the conclusion that he should ask for her hand in marriage.

So he left the same afternoon to go to the pot maker's home and speak to the poor pot maker, who was thrilled to see his daughter getting married to a wealthy king. But somehow his daughter didn't find King Alam to be very handsome, and she said to her father, "Do you know how old is he, Father? He looks old."

Her father replied, "He is thirty-eight now, but Amina, how often are you going to get a proposal for marriage from a king? Just think of all the joys you can have as a queen, and Alam's kingdom is one of the wealthiest ones."

Amina could not explain her inner feelings to her father. Her heart belonged to an ironsmith's son, who was twenty-seven years old but had well worked out body and was very handsome. She had been in love with him since the age of seventeen; in fact, he was the first man she had made love to. He loved her too; he was just waiting to save enough money to open his own ironsmith shop, where he could make farming tools, swords, and be financially independent enough to ask for her hand in marriage. Suddenly this King Alam had walked into her village to ruin all her dreams, her love life. How she had longed all those years to become Shamsher's wife, the wife of the best ironsmith in the entire village.

While she was still wrapped up in her thoughts, her father asked again, "Amina, Alam is waiting for your answer, and he wishes to marry you at once. What should I tell him?"

Amina thought quickly. This Alam is a powerful, wealthy king. If I refuse, he can declare war on our village. Knowing her village was too weak to fight against a strong king, so she would be taken by Alam with or without her consent, Amina decided instantly that she was not going to let some king ruin her love life. She said to her father, "If I am to marry Alam, he has to wait for three days, and I am allowed to bring a few of my female and male friends along with me to his kingdom and do as I please with them. Father, please find out whether he agrees to my terms."

When King Alam was told of Amina's conditions, he thought. Amina is young and perhaps wishes to bring her friends to my kingdom so she does not miss them or feel lonely. He agreed to Amina's terms at once and said, "I will visit one of my friend who is also a king who lives close to this village, and remain his guest for three days and make arrangements for my marriage."

Alam sent his soldiers away with hunted animals back to his kingdom. One soldier who had nominated himself to come along with Alam stayed back.

Alam left and got busy. He had the complete cooperation of King Shivram, who was pleased to have King Alam as his guest and also offered his full support for Alam's wedding. In the mean while Amina went and stayed with the ironsmith Shamsher, her lover, and explained her plans to him. He was to go with her and join Alam's army as a chief marshal, the top rank of the military, where he would have access to the king and queen's personal quarters. Whenever they found an opportune moment, they would make love with each other. Shamsher, as Alam's military marshal, was to get as many soldiers as possible on his side. When he had gathered enough military power, he was then to overthrow kingdom of Alam and become King Shamsher the owner of one of the wealthiest kingdoms in India.

Shamsher was always a cautious man; he didn't have much guts either. He knew this might sound easy to her, but it was not easy to rebel against one's own king without a spy finding out one's plans, and people who rebelled against their kings were tortured to death. He also knew Amina's plan might take a long time to accomplish. He didn't bother to tell Amina how risky all this might be, but he knew Amina was simply a beautiful young girl who was in love with him deeply; he loved her too, and he was willing to do whatever it took to be with her. So Shamsher agreed to go with Amina and asked three of his best friends to go with him. Amina picked out three of her good female friends who knew about her love for Shamsher and they said they would do anything and everything they could to help their friend Amina, who was suddenly going to become a powerful queen of one of the richest kingdoms. And few days before her marriage with Alam, Amina spent almost all night and most of the day making love with Shamsher.

Amina said to Alam, "I am too young for this uncomfortable horse ride. Arrange a carriage for me, and I will have Shamsher accompany me in it, as he is strong and fit and well-built to protect me. Go and arrange for my carriage at once."

Before Alam could utter even a word, Amina put her hand up and said, "Alam, what are you doing standing there and looking at me like that for? I asked you for a carriage. Now go this very moment, and do not return till you find me a nice, big, comfortable carriage attached to strong horses. I need this carriage to be built of the finest wood, with windows and a door and curtains, and the interior has to be of the finest, softest leather. Alam, I want you to know this: the sooner you understand my wishes, the better it is for you. I do not settle for anything less than the best. If you want me to become your wife and remain your wife, you better learn to fulfill my wishes at once and know that if I ever feel that you are giving me anything less than your best, I will leave you that moment."

To add salt to the wound, Amina looked in Alam's eyes and came very close to his face. Alam thought, "Oh, I am going to get a kiss after all. I am going be her husband tomorrow."

He had almost closed his eyes when he heard clearly, right in his ear, "Dismissed," and Amina turned around and walked away.

Alam's soldier was out getting water from the village's well otherwise he would be offended in the manner that Amina was treating Alam.

Alam was shocked. As he was walking toward his horse, he started thinking. Perhaps she is like this because she is young. My love will win her over, and she will learn some manners about how to talk to me and respect me. I am soon to be her husband. My love for her will win her love for me.

Alam went back to King Shivram and asked for a carriage along with some of his strong young horses. The carriage needed a little bit of work. More than fifteen carpenters along with bed makers put the carriage together in eight hours, and King Alam returned with a carriage custom made for his soon-to-be new wife.

But Amina was nowhere to be found. Alam asked Sheetal, a friend of Amina's, where she was, and Sheetal said, "She went to the river. I shall go and bring her."

"Do you want me to come with you?"

"No that won't be necessary."

The king said, "I will be waiting."

Sheetal found Amina making love with Shamsher under a mango tree on the riverbank. Amina was almost upset at her friend for spoiling her romantic lovemaking evening. Sheetal explained, "Alam is impatiently waiting for you. He sent me to bring you back. He wanted to come with me, but somehow I managed to convince him to stay."

Amina came back and asked Shamsher to return after fifteen minutes with some rabbits, as it would be the perfect excuse for him to be missing too. Shamsher, wasted no time and managed to hunt four rabbits, which were cooked and served for dinner. Alam was glad to see his Amina coming back and said, "It must be beautiful by the river. Would you like to go there with me and watch a beautiful sunset, Amina?"

Amina simply replied that she had done all her sightseeing for one day already. At her request, Shamsher was out hunting rabbits, and she would be delighted to eat her rabbit dinner and rest.

The next day Alam requested Amina take a shower and get ready, as the priest had been called and they were going to be married in the next hour. So Alam and Amina got married. The wedding was simple; Alam thought he would have a grand celebration in his own kingdom.

He thought perhaps dinner by the fire pit would please his wife, but he was soon to find out that his wife had eaten dinner with her friends and Shamsher and was ready to go to bed in her carriage. Alam ate alone and slept alone in his tent, hoping tomorrow would be a better day.

Upon sunrise they started heading back to Alam's kingdom. Time and time again, Alam's attempts to get any affection or love from his wife were turned down, but he thought perhaps once she was in his palace, she would start loving him. After five long days, they finally arrived at Alam's kingdom. Aurang was waiting with flowers, and the whole kingdom was decorated to welcome their new queen. Amina took a long, hard look at Aurang and said to Shamsher, who was sitting beside her in her luxurious carriage, "This is the man Alam is always talking so highly about. He seems to have some important part in Alam's life. We need to find out what. He also seems very wise and extremely good-looking man for barely being a king's advisor."

Upon the party's arrival in the kingdom, a grand wedding was arranged, and Alam felt he had married the most beautiful woman in the world. He showed his new queen all the private rooms of his palace. Her friends and Shamsher went wherever Alam and Amina went. The wedding dinner was elaborate. But Amina could not bear the fact that Alam was constantly trying to kiss her, hug her, and be affectionate toward her. She thought of a good excuse and said, "All this travel, visiting your vast kingdom, and going through the wedding celebrations has given me a big headache. I wish to rest now, Alam, and when I feel better, I will let you kiss me."

Amina knew she simply couldn't continue to put off Alam's attempts to kiss her and love her, and sooner or later, she would have to give in and allow Alam to make love to her, but she bought as much time as she could. Alam was disappointed, but he had no choice but to wait. After a long wait of a week, during which Amina always had some excuse to head off his advances, Alam could not take it anymore. He asked her, "Do you love me or at least like me, Amina? Are you happy to be my wife? Is there anything I can do for you to like me or love me?"

Amina realized that it could not be pushed any further, so she replied, "No, Alam, I am pleased to be your wife. It's just that I was not ready for marriage. I am so young; I know you have waited patiently for me. Come in my arms, and find out what you have been missing."

Alam and Amina made love. Alam was in heaven, but Amina was simply putting on a good show, thinking of Shamsher and eagerly waiting for it to be over.

The following day, Amina decided to go for a picnic with her female friends, and Shamsher was to go with her as her bodyguard. Amina explained to Shamsher how hard it was for her to make love to Alam and requested he come up with some plan to get rid of Alam soon. Amina always encouraged Alam to go on hunting trips and to visit distant kings. She requested gifts which were not locally available, and many times Alam had to travel for days to get to places to handpick gifts for his wife. As time went on, Shamsher could not become the best army general—he was simply an ironsmith and a very good lover, not much of a soldier—and hence taking over the kingdom was a distant dream.

Shamsher seemed to be content with the good life that he was living because of Amina, but Amina wanted to be the mother of his children; she wanted to be his wife, not Alam's, yet she saw that Shamsher did not have the will or courage to help her out of her situation, and she was forced to remain Alam's wife.

Alam's attempts to get Amina pregnant kept failing, as whenever Amina felt she was pregnant, she wondered if the child belonged to Shamsher or Alam, and she would send Sheetal to the royal doctor to get the medication for yet another abortion. Years were passing by and every time Alam thought his wife was pregnant, in the first or second month she would have a miscarriage. Upon Alam's request Amina went to doctor with Alam, but the doctor said, "There does not seem to be anything wrong with your wife."

Alam could not figure out why the miscarriages were happening.

Amina realized that her man Shamsher was not much of a soldier to overthrow or rebel against Alam. That was no longer an option, so she encouraged Shamsher to establish better ties with other kings in the hope that one of those kings would help overthrow Alam's kingdom and she and Shamsher could be together as king and queen.

Amina thought of a foolproof plan with King Hanuman Sign, with whom Shamsher seemed to be good friends. She had two letters written for King Hanuman, whose kingdom was less powerful than Alam's. The first letter simply read, "Whoever brings this letter to you from our kingdom should be beheaded and his body burned within your kingdom. Save the head as proof that he is dead. When this is done, the queen should be informed about it."

The second letter read, "Alam, who is bringing these two letters, is actually trying to team up with kings of other territories and is planning an invasion of King Hanuman's kingdom."

Shamsher, who liked King Hanuman, did not want any of this to happen, so this is what Queen Amina and Shamsher planned to do for King Hanuman as his good friends.

Amina asked Alam to take these two letters to the kingdom of Hanuman Sign. Alam had become accustomed to honoring Amina's wishes and dared not ask what was in the letters. He reached King Hanuman Sign's kingdom simply hoping to deliver the letters and pick up gifts for his wife upon his return. He was greeted at the main gates by the king himself and shown around and invited to have dinner with Hanuman. In deed King Hanuman's palace was very impressive. Dinner was served by a woman who had buckteeth, a big black mole on her chin, and a big scar on her left cheek; she wore very average-looking clothes. Suddenly, out of the blue, King Hanuman introduced Alam to this ugly woman as his wife.

"This is my wife, Komal Sign."

As soon as Komal left for the kitchen to start preparing dessert for her husband and their visitor, King Hanuman anxiously asked Alam, "So what do you think of my wife?"

On an impulse Alam wanted to say she was ugly and wearing such average clothes and barely fit the description of a servant; even Alam's servant looked better than this woman. But he remembered that Hanuman had said, "This is my wife, Komal sign,"

He remembered Azim's five lessons worth fifty thousand Rupees. The third lesson Azim had said, "You must show respect and appreciation for other people's choices."

So Alam simply said, "King Hanuman, she is so beautiful. She has such excellent facial features, and even in the dim light her beautiful figure showed so well. Besides her obvious looks, I am sure you must have seen good qualities in her that presently I am not aware of, for which you gladly married her."

King Hanuman asked Komal to come in the dining room right away and asked her to go wash her dark makeup off and change into her queen's clothes and come back. Alam was simply sitting there stunned, trying to figure out what was going on. King Hanuman spoke again in a very soft tone. "Alam, I do this with every new guest of mine. They all say that she does not look fit enough even to be my servant, that she is ugly with buckteeth and scar, and much harsher words, even after hearing that she is my wife. You are the first person who has had the wisdom to know the real beauty of a person lies inside him or her. You looked for what is truly beautiful about Komal instead of speaking as many other kings and my friends did when they were my guests."

When Komal returned in her queen's clothes and turned up the lights, the scar was washed away, the big black mole was gone, and the buckteeth were removed. She was indeed very beautiful, with light-blue eyes and pink lips and perfect facial features. It seemed like an angel had walked into Hanuman's dining room. Alam was mesmerized by Komal's beauty and said to Hanuman, "Indeed you have a very beautiful wife, Hanuman."

After dinner Alam was shown his guest room to rest for the night.

King Hanuman was getting ready to go to sleep. Before going to bed King Hanuman decided to open the confidential letters from Alam's wife that Alam had given to Hanuman upon coming to the palace to see what was written in these two letters. Hanuman could not believe what he was instructed to do in those letters: behead Alam and burn his body. Hanuman asked Komal for her advice, and Komal said, "Hanuman, Alam seems like a really nice person, and he is very wise. I am sure there is some kind of confusion somewhere. Why don't you spare his life? And please write a letter saying, 'I do not wish to kill Alam as per your request. I find him to be a very good human being and a very wise man. Amina, please give it serious thought before you decide to kill Alam. I am sure there is some kind of serious misunderstanding about Alam's intention to invade this kingdom, as I do not find Alam to be the type of king who would plot an invasion with help of other kings; his own kingdom is strong enough army-wise to take over my kingdom. Furthermore, if you wish to speak to me personally on the subject, I would be delighted to have you visit me, or I will come visit you.'"

While Alam was busy traveling to visit King Hanuman and bring back gifts for his wife which would never happen, as Alam was supposed to die on this trip Amina and Shamsher saw it as an opportunity for their romantic honeymoon time and ordered all servants to stay away from the private rooms of the palace. Only Shamsher's friends and Amina's friends from their own village were allowed to go there.

One afternoon Aurang wanted to get Amina to approve a weapons deal with a king from a nearby kingdom, as it was urgent and Alam was out of town. So Aurang, who had access to all of King Alam's palace, didn't bother to request permission but went straight to Amina's private bedroom. He saw Amina and Shamsher making love very passionately with each other, and they saw him watching them in bewilderment. Aurang could not believe his own eyes. He didn't know what to say or do. He was suspicious of Amina's alliance with Shamsher but simply thought Shamsher was a good childhood friend whom Amina had taken on as a good bodyguard. Aurang had no idea that the friendship between Amina and Shamsher was far more than just a friendship, that in fact they were lovers.

Aurang's right hand had already reached for the dagger that he always wore on his hip. He thought, how could Amina do this to his best friend? Such a bitch deserved to die. Aurang did not know he was capable of feeling such rage and anger inside him, but in that moment he remembered Azim's fourth and fifth lessons, which were about how to handle a difficult situation: Allah works in mysterious ways, and don't do anything when you are angry. So he simply excused himself and left them alone.

Amina and Shamsher knew that Aurang and Alam were good friends and that Aurang was Alam's advisor, and now this advisor had seen them making love in their complete nakedness, in the full heat of the moment. It had taken a few seconds for both Amina and Shamsher to even notice that Aurang was standing right at the bedroom door, watching them passionately making love.

Amina knew Aurang would speak to Alam and her and Shamsher's great love affair would come to an end. Once Alam found out Shamsher was Amina's lover, Alam would have Shamsher tortured to death. One such torture was to pierce a man's genitals and bladder with iron hooks attached to metal chains, each chain connecting to a larger chain tied to an elephant's chest. The elephant was instructed to walk slowly, halting often, from the kingdom's main gate to the royal palace. The person being tortured was completely nude and died very painfully while the people of the kingdom were invited to watch this, learning the lesson never to mess around with the king's wife.

At the same time, Amina thought, with what had been written in those letters to King Hanuman, Alam might not even return from this trip. Once Alam was dead, the soldiers could be ordered to capture Aurang and kill him too.

In the mean time it was very hard for Aurang to address his queen with respect, and he avoided any kind of interaction with Shamsher. Aurang noticed Amina was more impolite and rude toward him, and they all seemed to ignore the whole episode altogether.

Amina was waiting eagerly to see King Hanuman's men bring the letter containing the good news that Alam was dead, so she was extremely disappointed to see King Alam return on his horse with the requested gifts and a letter for her from King Hanuman. As soon as Amina was able to, she met Shamsher and told him about Alam's safe arrival, and they both were eager to read King Hanuman's letter together.

Amina and Shamsher walked to the royal garden. Amina's first instinct was to think of what to say to Alam in the event Aurang decided to tell him about Amina and Shamsher being lovers. Amina knew that all the other royal servants had been asked to stay away from her private bedroom, which meant there were no other witnesses, which meant she could prove Aurang was lying, and she was already fabricating the story in her head. Amina would simply say to her husband that even though there were orders not to enter Queen Amina's private chambers, Aurang had walked into the queen's bedroom in the afternoon, while she was in the shower, and seeing Amina completely nude, the beast inside of Aurang woke up. He was no longer thinking with his right head and had tried to rape Amina, but luckily Shamsher, her bodyguard, had heard her cry for help and come to her rescue before Aurang could rape her.

Amina sat in the royal garden next to her lover to read Hanuman's letter.

Hanuman letter to Amina said, 'I do not wish to kill Alam as per your request. I find him to be a very good human being and a very wise man. Amina, please give it serious thought before you decide to kill Alam. I am sure there is some kind of serious misunderstanding about Alam's intention to invade this kingdom, as I do not find Alam to be the type of king who would plot an invasion with help of other kings; his own kingdom is strong enough army-wise to take over my kingdom. Furthermore, if you wish to speak to me personally on the subject, I would be delighted to have you visit me, or I will come visit you.'"

They both were thinking of how to eliminate Alam. Suddenly Shamsher came up with a plan. He said, "There is an assassin who is very famous and known for his willingness to kill without asking many questions. He cares only about money. He charges five thousand Rupees per kill."

Amina said, "Money won't be a problem. I just have to get to Alam's safe, where he keeps all the royal treasury, jewels, and money."

Shamsher said, "How are we going to do this, Amina?"

Amina thought of yet another foolproof plan. This time the assassin was to wait at the main gate of Alam's kingdom, and whoever went out of that gate at sunrise would be killed and beheaded and his head left in the middle of the main gate for the next person who went there to find. Amina then said, "Sweetheart you will go there next and bring me Alam's head."

This did not require any hand drawn pictures, as Shamsher was sure if an assassin saw King Alam's hand drawn picture, he would ask for more money, and if he knew he was about to kill the king, he might refuse to do the job. Shamsher would arrange for the money to reach the assassin through one of his trusted friend; Along with instructions for the assassin this way the assassin wouldn't even know what Shamsher looked like. Shamsher was covering his tracks. All the assassin had to do was kill the first man who came out of Alam's kingdoms main gate right at sunrise. Once Alam was dead, they would figure out a way to kill Aurang.

Aurang thought about the whole situation with Amina and Shamsher long and hard and wanted to talk to Alam about it, but he remembered Azim's five lessons worth fifth thousand Rupees, and the fourth lesson in particular: "Many times in our lives, we are presented with situations that we do not know how to handle. It is always good to use our best judgment during these trying times. Sometimes it's better simply to leave it alone, as Allah has a way of working things out mysteriously."

So Aurang said to himself I will allow Allah to work this one out. He knew how much Alam loved Amina, and he could not bear to be the one to give such bad news to the king. He decided that since Amina and Shamsher were lovers, sooner or later Alam would catch them red handed, as Aurang had, and that would be the end of it. So he decided not to do anything about it.

So came a day when once again Amina asked Alam to go to a nearby kingdom and bring her jewels that were being sold at a fair there. Amina said specifically, "I want you to leave few minutes before sunrise and be the first one to leave our kingdom, as these ear rings are rare and might get sold, so you should be the first one to get them for me, be the first customer when this jewelry seller opens."

A number of times Alam suggested that a king's man or a soldier would be happy to pick up these gifts for Amina, but Amina simply said, "If they do it for you, it is because you are a king. I do not feel so special, because before becoming a queen I lived an average woman's life, where anyone who cared for me, like my friends or my father, would get gifts for me themselves, and that made me feel special. Besides, don't you love me enough to do something as simple as go to a fair and pick up a pair of simple but rare earrings for your wife?"

Amina had a way of manipulating things and liked winning conversations, and Alam knew better than to offend her because that would mean she would stop sleeping in the same bedroom as he and would treat him rudely on regular basis, which he hated. So he came to terms with it, knowing he had better do whatever Amina asked him to do. It had become common for Amina to ask Alam to go out of town every week or so. So Alam agreed to leave early the following morning.

That night Amina even made love with Alam with some passion while thinking Alam, tonight is your last night on planet earth. An assassin is waiting to kill you tomorrow morning. She kept looking at him carefully, knowing she will never see this face alive, come tomorrow morning. Alam was so happy to get so much attention from his wife in bed that he simply kept telling her how much he loved her, and how he longed to be a father of their child, and how he would always love her and would never leave her and would never let anyone or anything hurt her in any way.

Amina and Alam made love till the wee hours of the night. Alam finally went to bed at two am and Amina went to take a shower in her private queen's quarters, where Shamsher was waiting for her, as he was missing her very much. Amina was tired, but Shamsher was the love of her life, so as always, Shamsher and Amina made love. Amina could not help but think that Shamsher was a much better lover and made love to her the way she liked it, rough. Amina went to sleep at six am, just before Alam could wake up. She quietly went to the other side of bed and lay down.

Alam woke up at six thirty almost in a panic, as his wife had asked him to leave before sunrise: "At the first ray of sunlight I want you to be at the main gate."

So Alam hurriedly got dressed, while he was still riding his horse as fast as he could, the sun began to shine. As he reached the gate, he saw someone being killed. Alam rushed over as quickly as he could, but the assassin vanished into the thick bushes in the forest outside the main gates of the kingdom. Alam didn't even get to look at the assassin's face.

As Alam came closer to the dead body, which was lying lifeless in the middle of the gate, with its head a few feet away from the body, he suddenly realized that it was Shamsher. He wondered if Shamsher had enemies and also what Shamsher was doing so early in the morning by the main gate. He had never known him to wake before ten or eleven. Alam knew how much Amina liked Shamsher as her bodyguard, and now Alam would have to hire someone new to be her bodyguard. He found a soldier who was guarding the gate from inside and asked for the body to be carried to the palace.

Just then Aurang was riding out of the palace to go to meet a stone carver, as he was planning to give a life-size statue to Alam on his wedding anniversary, which was a month away. It takes a while for a stone carver to finish a job, and stone carvers usually leave early to go looking for stones to work with, so Aurang knew leaving early would ensure his meeting with the stone carver. When he noticed Alam at the gate, he was bit surprised, as he didn't know if Alam was going out again to bring gifts for Amina. He knew Amina always kept Alam busy, but somehow this morning was different. A soldier brought in the dead body of Shamsher, whom Aurang knew as Amina's lover. Aurang asked Alam, "If he knew who had killed Shamsher, how he had died, and whether Amina knew Shamsher was dead?"

Now all Aurang wanted to do was to see how Amina reacted to her lover's death, so he requested to come along with Alam.

Amina was asleep when her servant woke her up to give her news of Shamsher's death. Amina was still half-awake. She was tired from making love to King Alam till two o'clock and some more with Shamsher till six. Exhausted, she hardly paid any attention to what the servant was saying and said, "I am very tired. How dare you disturb me so early in the morning? I am going right back to bed. I will hear what you have to say to me later."

As soon as Amina opened her eyes to see which servant dared to disturb her so she could have her fired the next day, she saw the servant was holding Shamsher's head on a silver platter, put there by Aurang's request. Shamsher's face looked dead lifeless scary in a way, his body lying lifeless on the floor in white sheets with bloodstains on them. Amina screamed, "No! This can't happen! Alam, you were the one who was supposed to die. No, Shamsher, you can't leave me alone with this hideous, pathetic Alam who does not even know how to please a woman in bed. Shamsher, who killed you, my Shamsher?"

Amina was crying hysterically.

Alam was shocked to see Amina in this state; he could hardly believe anything she was saying.

This time King Aurangzeb decided to break the silence and spoke with his usual kingly authoritative voice. He spoke to Amina. "Stop crying, you slut, and shut up and listen to me."

Amina could barely believe her ears and asked Alam, "Alam, did your advisor just call me a slut?"

Alam, who was still in shock over how his wife had called him pathetic, could not say anything. There was too much happening at once. Aurangzeb spoke again and said, "Amina never loved you, Alam. In fact, she loved Shamsher, and he was her lover all along. I even saw them making love to each other while you were out visiting King Hanuman last month."

Aurangzeb spoke to Amina again and said, "Amina, I am King Aurangzeb, from the kingdom of Aurangabad. Azim wanted me to implement lessons of wisdom in practical life, Amina you don't need to know who Azim is? so I set off with my advisor, Alamgir, whom you know as Alam. I don't need to tell you the details of our lessons and what we came here to learn, but Alamgir is my advisor and a trustworthy friend, and he considers me his valuable friend as well. Now you answer my question: How did Shamsher, your lover, turn up dead?"

Amina looked hopelessly at Alamgir for help. Alamgir, looking directly at Amina, said, "Everything Aurangzeb said is absolute truth."

Amina noticed the irony of the situation and acknowledged the fact that King Aurangzeb was really the king, as Alam had shown genuine respect for Aurang all along and rarely did anything without asking Aurang first. She begged her life be spared and she would speak the whole truth. King Aurangzeb said, "Yes, your life will be spared. Now go on. Speak the whole truth."

Amina explained to both Alamgir and Aurangzeb that she had loved Shamsher since the age of seventeen and he was the first man she ever made love to. King Alam's wedding invitation had messed up their love affair, but she feared refusing a powerful king's marriage offer, as it could be implemented with or without her consent. On the other hand, Amina knew becoming a queen was not something that happened every day and thought Shamsher would become a powerful general and overthrow King Alam, but that didn't happen. Since she was sleeping with her lover and her husband at the same time, she could not tell whose child she was pregnant with, so she would simply have an abortion and say she had yet another miscarriage. She couldn't take it anymore; hence she plotted to send Alam with two letters to King Hanuman.

The first letter simply read, "Whoever brings this letter to you from our kingdom should be beheaded and his body burned within your kingdom. Save the head as proof that he is dead. When this is done, the queen should be informed about it."

The second letter read, "Alam, who is bringing these two letters, is actually trying to team up with kings of other territories and is planning an invasion of King Hanuman's kingdom."

But instead of killing Alam, the king Hanuman had replied "I do not wish to kill Alam as per your request. I find him to be a very good human being and a very wise man. Amina, please give it serious thought before you decide to kill Alam. I am sure there is some kind of serious misunderstanding about Alam's intention to invade this kingdom, as I do not find Alam to be the type of king who would plot an invasion with help of other kings; his own kingdom is strong enough army-wise to take over my kingdom. Furthermore, if you wish to speak to me personally on the subject, I would be delighted to have you visit me, or I will come visit you."

"While Alam was visiting Hanuman, Aurang caught me red handed making love passionately with Shamsher in our complete nakedness. I was sure Aurang would tell you and had planned my defense. I would have twisted the story by saying Aurang was trying to rape me but Shamsher, my bodyguard, came in time to save me from being raped. I am good at manipulating things. I am sure Alam, being helplessly in love with me, would have believed me over Aurang's story. But for some reason Alam continued loving me, which made me think maybe Aurang did not have the courage to ruin his king's happiness, or whatever the reason might have been. So when my first plan flopped, I created a second one. I hired an assassin, who was paid for by Shamsher's friends. This assassin did not ask questions but charged five thousand Rupees per kill. His instructions were to kill the first person who came out of the kingdoms main gate at sunrise."

Amina explained that Shamsher was supposed to go collect the head of Alam, but she also explained the assassin's role and that what must have happened was that King Alam was running late. Shamsher had gone to see if Alam was dead already, but the assassin had no clue whom he was supposed to kill other than the fact that whoever came out of the main gate of Alam's kingdom at sunrise. Shamsher happened to be the first one there, so he got himself killed.

Amina said, "I am simply a woman in love with another man. If only kings would ask women if they really want to marry them instead of throwing their authority around, which makes simple people like me scared, knowing if I refuse to marry a king, he might get upset and kill my lover or kill me, abduct me, and take me with him against my wishes. Anything is possible for a king. I had no idea what kind of a king Alam is. All I knew was Alam fancied me and wanted to marry me at once."

Alamgir saw how it all had played out and was very sad to know the woman he loved for the last five years had never even loved him. He was heartbroken. Aurangzeb named Amina's poor pot maker father the next king of Jhansi and allowed Amina to remain as queen. He had Amina sign a treaty saying that Amina and her father would never attack King Aurangzeb's kingdom and would always help in any shape or form if need ever arose. Amina agreed to all these terms, knowing very well that Aurangzeb and Alamgir could have easily had her killed. After all, King Aurangzeb and Alamgir had just forgiven her for trying to kill them and for playing these types of horrible games with them.

Aurangzeb was riding on his horse heading back to his kingdom Aurangabad. A few of the soldiers from Jhansi decided to go with Aurangzeb and Alamgir, and on the journey Aurangzeb realized that it had been five years since he had last seen his wife. He wondered if she had married some-one else or waited for him, and how would she re-act when she sees him? It was late at night when they reached the kingdom's gates. Alamgir suggested spending few hours of late night in the tents and entering the Aurangabad kingdom the next morning, but King Aurangzeb was very eager to meet his wife, so he decided to keep going.

Aurangzeb and Alamgir reached the gates of their kingdom. A senior sol-dier recognized King Aurangzeb at once, and he was very happy to see his king return after all these years. When King Aurangzeb reached the private quarters of his wife, it was almost five am. He went inside the queen's bedroom and in the dim light saw his wife, looking as beautiful as when he had seen her last. Lying right next to her was a young man, he looked eighteen years old but well worked out body and very handsome, even while sleeping. King Aurangzeb thought while I was away for five years, my wife, being a queen, got in the habit of sleeping with young, handsome men. She is a queen, so she can do as she pleases, especially as her husband, the king, has been gone for so many years.

But he still could not bear the fact that his wife and this man were sleeping in the same bed that he used to sleep in with her. He reached for his sword and pulled it out. As he was walking toward the young man to kill him, Alamgir, who was passing by, noticed Aurangzeb was holding a sword and ready to kill someone. Alamgir quickly ran and stepped right in between Aurangzeb and the handsome young man, who was still sleeping. Alamgir said to Aurangzeb, "Remember that the third lesson of the wise man helped save my life with King Hanuman. The fifth and last lesson of Azim was never to do anything when you are angry. I know it is hard. I wanted to kill Amina, but you spared her life. I was very upset and angry with Amina at the time, Aurangzeb, but I let it go, and said to myself, 'The ability to forgive is greater than the ability to punish.' Why don't we wait right outside Queen Dilraz's room and talk to her later on when she wakes up? Where are they going to go? This is the only door to get in and out. I will have the windows guarded by our trusted soldiers with swords so that this young man does not escape."

It was very difficult for Aurangzeb, but he was experiencing the same rage and anger that he had experienced when he caught Amina and Shamsher naked, making love to each other. He decided to implement Azim's fifth lesson never do anything when you are angry simply drink lots of water and get yourself to calm down so he requested a big jar of cold water.

Queen Dilraz woke up at six am and pulled the shades open and said, "Mazuddin, my dear son, wake up. Today you have to go for your army training. Don't you wish to impress your father when he returns and show him all your weaponry skills?"

Mazuddin, who was still sleepy, said, "Mother, you talk about my father's coming home every day, but he never comes, and you don't even know if remembers us, if he is still alive?"

Dilraz put her hand on his mouth almost right away and said, "Son, my heart tells me he is alive, and he will come home someday. Now get ready for your army training."

Aurangzeb, who was still standing in the doorway, heard all this. He ran in the bedroom and picked up Dilraz and hugged her and kissed her on her cheek. Dilraz saw Aurangzeb was right there in front of her very eyes. She noticed he was more elegant and handsome than ever. Dilraz screamed to her son, "Come here, Mazuddin. Get out of the bathroom, and meet your father at once."

Mazuddin, who was getting ready to brush his teeth, threw the toothbrush away, and came running in the bedroom and saw his father after five years. He came closer and hugged his father and said, "Mother always said how handsome my father is. I didn't remember much as a young kid, but now I believe it so much more because I see you, Father. You look so elegantly handsome."

Aurangzeb said his son, "You, look wonderful, like a young prince, and very handsome yourself."

While Mazuddin was in the bathroom taking a shower, King Aurangzeb explained to Dilraz how he had wanted to kill Mazuddin but how Alamgir had stopped him and explained Azim's fifth lesson, which had saved the life of his own son. He requested the servants serve breakfast. As soon as Mazuddin's training was done. Which Aurangzeb, Dilraz, and Alamgir watched, they all agreed that Mazuddin was surely doing a great job learning skills on various weapons and would be a great king soon.

It was a beautiful sunny day. Aurangzeb decided to have lunch in the royal garden with his family. Just before lunch was served, Aurangzeb started talking about Azim's five lessons worth fifty thousand Rupees and how they had saved the lives of both Alamgir and Aurangzeb. Dilraz felt bad for Alamgir as she could see he really loved Amina; she felt sad that Amina could not love him back. Dilraz said politely to Aurangzeb, her husband, "Sweetheart, my cousin's sister is turning thirty this year. Her name is Mumtaz. Her husband died a few years ago in a hunting accident, and she has a good upbringing. If it is okay with you, Alamgir, I could talk to her parents to arrange for your wedding with her."

Alamgir was blushing, as he had seen Mumtaz as a young girl and knew she must have grown up to be a beautiful woman. Alamgir asked Dilraz, "Does she have any children?"

Dilraz replied, "No."

Alamgir said, "Would it be okay if I wished to meet her before we extend a marriage proposal?"

Dilraz said, "I can arrange a meeting as soon as possible."

Alamgir agreed. Mazuddin, who was listening to the whole conversation, quietly said, "Father, with your permission, can I go with mother to aunty Mumtaz's kingdom? I have never traveled that far, and it would be a wonderful opportunity for me to see the world outside the walls of our kingdom."

Aurangzeb was surprised to know his son had never stepped foot outside his kingdom, and he asked Dilraz, "How come, my son never been outside our fort walls?"

Dilraz said, "Mazuddin is your son, Aurangzeb, and he was all I had for five years till you came back today. Besides, I wanted to be a very protective mother for him. I would not have been able to show you my face had anything happened to Mazuddin."

Aurangzeb saw her point and said, "Son, now that you have learned the art of weaponry so wonderfully, I am sure nothing can hurt you. My son, you have my permission to go with your mother."

Mazuddin was excited to see the outside world and said to Dilraz excitedly, "Mother, can we leave at once?"

Dilraz said, "Aurangzeb, your father and I have not been with each other for five long years. Don't you think we deserve to spend at least one whole day together? Mazuddin, you and I will leave tomorrow morning. Is that alright? my son?"

Mazuddin agreed. Lunch was being served. Dilraz had the cooks make eggplant because that was Aurangzeb's favorite dish. Dilraz had done a great job of maintaining Aurangzeb's vast kingdom. During the day both Aurangzeb and Alamgir looked at the important paperwork regarding the kingdom. Dilraz's most important project was to make a man-made lake for irrigation in the kingdom, as rain was never a sure thing. Aurangzeb and Alamgir decided to go and look at the lake site and also start working on it right away.

The next day Mazuddin and Dilraz left to meet with Mumtaz's parents. Mazuddin was ready early in the morning. Aurangzeb said to Dilraz, "Be careful, dear, as you will be passing through some thick forest."

Dilraz said, "I am also taking five soldiers with me. I should be safe."

Dilraz returned with Mumtaz and her parents, who were very anxious to meet their new son-in-law, Alamgir. When Alamgir saw Mumtaz, he was awestruck. Mumtaz had long, straight silky black hair, high cheekbones, pink lips, the most beautiful kind hazel eyes, and a slender figure, and she looked like an angel in long light-blue dress that was well stitched, showing her feminine figure very well. Alamgir had learned from his previous experience not to assume that a woman found him to be her perfect suitor, so this time he decided to have an in-depth conversation with Mumtaz first.

Alamgir said to Mumtaz, "Hello, my name is Alamgir, and I am a royal advisor for Aurangzeb. I also consider myself Aurangzeb's and his family's trusted friend. Would you be so kind as to accompany me for a short walk in the royal garden?"

As he was saying this, he also looked at Aurangzeb to seek his approval, and Aurangzeb gave a big smile and gestured for Alamgir to carry on. Mumtaz quickly stepped alongside Alamgir and started walking toward the garden. She said to Alamgir in a very soft and kind voice, "My name is Mumtaz Banu. My parents had me complete all of my education. Soon after my education was done, I was married to Jhangir, my late husband. He was a wealthy land-lord, well respected and a very noble, kind man of his village. He loved hunt-ing, adventure, and wilderness. On a hunting trip he was bitten by a king cobra, and since the location was remote, isolated in the mountains, he was unable to get medical attention in time; hence he lost his life. I was married when I was twenty-seven years old, and my marriage lasted only six months. I have received many offers for marriage since then, but I refused them, as I was unable to get over my late husband. Most of these marriage offers were from random men, merchants, landlords, even two different kings, first king wanted me as his third wife, second king was almost sixty years old, but I always refused, as I didn't know much about them, and the more I found out, the less I was interested. I was able to hear about their arrogance, their nega-tive pride. One marriage offer came from a man who was sixty-five years old. I had almost given up on the idea of marriage when Dilraz, my cousin, came along and explained how you were such a faithful husband to an unfaithful wife and how Dilraz, Aurangzeb, and Mazuddin trust you wholeheartedly. When I saw your hand drawn painting, Alamgir, I could not help but notice your good looks. You look lot better than any other man I have known. I am sure you have been told that before. So my parents and I decided at once to come and meet you, and here I am, talking your ears off. I have been told I talk too much, but Alamgir, if you have further questions, please ask. I don't lie, and I strongly dislike liars."

Alamgir was scared about the age gap between them and said to Mumtaz, "We do have a bit of an age gap between us. I worry about that."

Mumtaz replied, "Love is all you need. Age is only a number."

By this time Alamgir knew Mumtaz was the one for him.

So Alamgir and Mumtaz decided to get married the same week. Alamgir asked Aurangzeb to be the guest of honor at the wedding, as Aurangzeb was indeed a very charming man. On the day of Alamgir's wedding, Aurangzeb was busy trying to get the best gift for his best friend and was busy making sure the dinner reception was up to par. The women were busy doing the flowers, and Mazuddin had arranged for an indoor wildlife show, where vari-ous exotic animals were brought in from all over the other kingdoms.

While everyone was busy, Azimuddin walked in Aurangabad kingdoms gates and spoke to the soldier at the gate with his obvious confidence, he was brought to King Aurangzeb's private quarters. Azim had a beautiful wife, two sons, and a daughter with him. When he saw King Aurangzeb, he greeted the king with the same charm and confidence and calmness that he always seemed to have. "Hello, Aurangzeb. It's been less than two weeks since you are back from kingdom of Jhansi, and Alamgir is already getting married to Mumtaz Banu. Aurangzeb, I am disappointed in you and Alamgir that I didn't receive an invitation to Alamgir's wedding. Nevertheless, I didn't think I would need an invitation to come and meet with you. I took the liberty of inviting myself, along with my family, to Alamgir's wedding. Let me introduce you to my lovely wife, Zahera, my sons, Salim and Shahid, and my little star daughter, Zaina."

Aurangzeb felt awful for forgetting to invite Azim, then he said, "Azim, all this happened so quickly it slipped my mind to send a wedding invitation to you, I am sorry Azim."

Aurangzeb was Astonished to see that Azim knew he was in Jhansi for past 5 years and return to his own kingdom only two weeks ago, not just that he knows Alamgir is getting married and he even knows the name of Alamgir's soon-to-be-wife's name as well.

Aurangzeb said to Azim, "I am so glad, Azim, that you decided to grace Alamgir with your presence at his wedding. I am sure he will be equally happy to meet you and your family. Let me show you a private room where you and your family can freshen up."

As they started walking toward the king's private quarters, Mazuddin came running. "Father, Father, what would you like me to wear for Alamgir's wedding? I have these three choices. Mother thinks I should wear this blue dress. I personally like this dark blue color dress, and I know you like a black-and-white combination, so I picked up this black dress with a white shirt and a black collar."

As he was carrying all three hangers with clothes in his hands, he noticed his father was with an impressive-looking man who had a beautiful woman standing by his side and three most beautiful-looking kids. Mazuddin suddenly realized perhaps his father was busy with some important people from the wedding and that he had interrupted him. He almost immediately apologized. "I am sorry, Father. In my excitement I didn't notice that you were busy with wedding guests."

That was when Aurangzeb introduced Mazuddin to Azim and his family.

Mazuddin had faint memories of meeting Azim for the first time when he was eleven years old then again when he was thirteen years old and now he is meeting him again formally introduced by this father at the age of eighteen years old.

Mazuddin, with his boyish charm, quickly said in a joking manner, "Oh, so you are the one that kept my father away from me for last five years. Well, you helped him make so much money with your pearl trick. My mother told me so many good things about you. It is my honor to finally formally being introduced to you and meet you, Azimuddin."

As soon as Azim and his family were shown their private guest rooms, Mazuddin was still waiting to hear what dress his father wanted him to wear for Alamgir's wedding. Aurangzeb said, "Wear the dark blue color dress. That dress fits you well, and you look most handsome in it. Now that I have helped you with your clothes, let's walk together in the royal garden for a brief talk."

Mazuddin quickly had the servant take his clothes to his room and started walking alongside his father. Aurangzeb said, "Son, I am very proud of you for learning all about the army and weapons and for being the best horse rider in our kingdom. You swim every day and work out three times a week, and you are well built, 5'11, almost six feet tall, very strong, and a very intelligent, very handsome young man with eager charm, a bit of overexcitement or perhaps lack of patience. But you are young, and sometimes young people think nothing is impossible. Son, being confident is good, but being overconfident is not good. I noticed you have not bothered to ask me about Azim's five lessons in detail."

Mazuddin, who was working on being a good listener, said, "Father, if you don't mind, may I say something?"

Aurangzeb said, "Go ahead and say it."

Mazuddin then said, "Ever since I was eleven years old, Mother always told me how you ran into Azim 'Have brain but no money,' which brought you lots of wealth and, within two years of that, five lessons worth fifty thousand Rupees. In a way I wish Azim had not chosen your kingdom to do that. Knowing you are curious by nature, he played on it, and you bought into it, but all this caused me to grow up without a father by my side for last five years, so I am a bit resentful toward Azim. This is why I did not ask you in detail about those five lessons. But I understand you respect him; I saw that in your eyes when I walked up to you with three dresses in my arms."

Aurangzeb realized it was a bit selfish of him to have stayed away from his wife and son for so many years. He apologized at once to Mazuddin for not being there for all his young age, but he quickly went on to say that had he not followed Azim's five lessons, he would not have been able to have this conversation with his son.

He explained quickly how the last five years had gone by. Upon leaving their own kingdom, Alamgir had become a king and he an advisor. The first letter from Amina to King Hanuman had said, "Kill the person who brings this letter to you,"

But Alamgir had saved his neck by implementing the third lesson and admiring King's Hanuman's wife in old beat-up clothes. Using the fourth lesson Aurangzeb had saved Alamgir's and his own life by not talking about Amina and her lover Shamsher, and the fifth lesson, "Never do anything when you are angry."

Had saved Mazuddin himself from the Aurangzeb's sword. Aurangzeb had been furious, but Alamgir had remembered the fifth lesson and insisted he wait until morning to kill Mazuddin, after asking the queen about it, of course. "So now you see, son, sometimes just implementing what we know to be true can be the only difference between life and death."

Aurangzeb continued talking to Mazuddin. "Son, your heart is in the left side of your chest, but it is always right. Listen to it, and you and your life won't go wrong. Mazuddin, I know you have many things to do. This evening is Alamgir's wedding with Mumtaz. I won't keep you all evening long. You are free to run along."

When Mazuddin was ready to leave, Aurangzeb said, "Are you forgetting something, Mazuddin?"

Mazuddin quickly came closer and gave his father a big hug and a kiss on his cheek and said, "I love you, Father."

Aurangzeb said, "I love you too, my son."

Azim, who had become a very wealthy businessman over the years, decided to feed the entire Kingdom of Aurangzeb wonderfully cooked an elaborate dinner the following day and even arranged for beautiful fireworks after the wedding as a gift for Alamgir. In deed it was the most amazing fireworks King Aurangzeb and his kingdom had ever seen. And they all lived happily ever after.

Majid's father continued on to his next story. It was past eleven o'clock. Majid was feeling very sleepy, but he was thoroughly enjoying these stories, which his father had never told him before. So he stayed awake and paid attention to his father's stories.

CHAPTER 5

Wali's Five Weeks of Lessons

Majid's father won't stop talking and telling him one story after another. Having finished three stories, he starts a fourth, a continuation about Mazuddin.

"Once there was an actual miracle-worker named Wali Sahib who ran his own small education home called "Samajdar boarding school" where he would teach five students at any given time. Each student had his own rooms with attached toilets. And two servants to maintain this education home."

Majid's father paused and asked, "Do you remember the earlier three stories my son?"

Majid replied, "Yes, Abbu Ji."

Then his father went on to talk about Wali Sahib and how a king's son, Mazuddin, had been asked to go there by his father, to Wali's Samajdar boarding school.

Now Mazuddin was thinking, "Happily ever after" only existed in fairy tales. It was just thirty-five days ago in his father's kingdom, Aurangabad, where his father, Aurangzeb, had returned shortly before Mazuddin's eighteenth birthday. What a happy time that had been, celebrating Alamgir's wedding to Mumtaz in the company of Azimuddin.

Mazuddin was enjoying all the privileges of a young prince destined to become a king someday. And now, sitting on the lonesome beach weeping these past two hours, he was replaying a conversation he'd had earlier this evening with Azimuddin.

Azimuddin had told him, "Three kings from surrounding territories of Aurangabad combined their army forces and attacked your father's kingdom with many horses and elephants as well as with thousands of marching soldiers. Your father, Aurangzeb, who was recovering from malaria, was still weak. He had never fought any battle or war and was badly defeated by King Kansa from the Varanasi Kingdom. Aurangzeb was forced to watch his wife - your mother - brutally killed in front of him. Next were Alamgir and his pregnant wife Mumtaz.

When Kansa was ready to cut off your father's head he asked, "Do you have any last wish?"

Aurangzeb said, "Please spare my son's life."

Surprised, Kansa said, "Oh, I didn't know you have a son. Thank you for informing me. I have learned from other people's mistakes as well as my own never to leave any relative of the person you are killing alive, as they may grow up to become stronger than I am, and come back someday seeking revenge when I am least expecting it."

The next question Kansa asked was, "Where is your son?"

Aurangzeb, knowing well that indeed he had unknowingly put his only son's life in danger, said to Kansa, "You might as well kill me because I love my son more than my own life, so I will not tell you."

They tortured your father for days and nights but he wouldn't talk. After five days of torture and without any food or water, on fifth day King Kansa beheaded your father.

However, while your father was still alive and in the darkness of the night, one soldier was able to come to Aurangzeb's jail room and bring some water with him.

The soldier said, "Kansa's night guard has fallen asleep, so I am risking my own life to bring you some water, King Aurangzeb."

Aurangzeb asked, "What is your name, brave soldier?"

He replied, "Ajaz."

Aurangzeb then said, "Ajaz, thank you for bringing me the water. Without medication for malaria and before I can fully recover, I'm being slowly killed. Along with Kansa's tortures, and lack of nutrition or food and water, I know I am surely going to die, maybe in a day to two. Now listen carefully to me. I have a favor to ask from you."

Ajaz answered right away, "My life is yours, sir. Ask me for whatever you need."

Aurangzeb spoke softly, making sure no one would overhear him. Ajaz brought his face closer to the dying king so he could hear correctly.

"Inside our royal garden is a fountain. There is an angel who is standing with a water pot, the water flows through the pot. Do you remember seeing the angel in my garden with the water pot?"

Ajaz answered, "Yes." He remembered it was a most beautiful angel carved out of marble stone.

Relieved that the soldier knew about the angel, Aurangzeb continued with his directions. "You'll notice she is holding the pot with her left hand. Pulling on the right hand activates and opens up the grass beds behind the fountain. Follow the tunnel which leads all the way out of my Aurangabad kingdom. It goes many miles and opens by Lake Limbe Jalgoan and into a dense forest. We have paved a small path with white pebbles from the opening of this tunnel that leads out to the city of Kadim Shahpur.

"Once inside the tunnel, you'll see an angel holding a torch in her right hand. Pull on the left hand of the angel to close the tunnel behind you. As soon as the tunnel closes, all the torches automatically light up from one end to the other where this tunnel ends. Had I known my army and other defenses were so weak, I would have taken the tunnel and led my wife, Alamgir, Mumtaz, and myself out of harm's way.

"Unfortunately, Kansa won the war in less than half an hour, and before I could leave the battle field. Being in the early stages of recovery from malaria didn't help either. Everything happened so fast I didn't even get a chance to escape with my wife, and Alamgir and Mumtaz. Kansa caught up with me, and you know the rest."

Aurangzeb took out the pen and paper hidden inside his coat pocket, quickly wrote a note, and handed it to Ajaz saying, "Here is the address of Azimuddin. You may or may not know him, but he is the one who arranged spectacular fireworks for Alamgir's wedding. He lives in Kadim Shahpur. Please tell him about my misfortune so he can go to the school of Wali Sahib where my son Mazuddin is currently studying. He is to advise Mazuddin to leave India before Kansa's men find and kill him, too.

"Please be very careful around the garden as Kansa should not know about this tunnel, and please don't get caught escaping. That would put your life further at risk. I will die thankful to you Ajaz."

Ajaz replied, "Sir, I remember seeing Azimuddin with his wife and kids. I will go and deliver this urgent message, and I will be very careful."

As soon as Ajaz located Azimuddin and delivered the king's handwritten message, he returned to the tunnel, made his way back to Aurangabad, and re-united with his fellow soldiers.

Azimuddin recognized the urgency of Aurangzeb's message. He rushed to Wali Sahib's Samajdar boarding school, and before talking to Mazuddin, Azimuddin had a detailed talk with Wali Sahib describing Mazuddin's situation.

Wali said, "Allah works in mysterious ways. Only Allah knows the reasons why things happen the way they do. Mazuddin is busy packing his bags to return to his parents as his five week's school just ended today. A servant will take you to his room."

Azimuddin followed the servant, greeted Mazuddin, and showed him the note from his father. He explained how the courageous soldier Ajaz had spent two days traveling through the long tunnel without much water or food in order to deliver his father's note.

Azimuddin spoke extensively to Mazuddin saying, "Toward the end of the tunnel Ajaz pulled on the hand of another angel. The tunnel gate opened to a grassy forest floor. He was trying to figure out how to close those gates behind him when he spied a small stone angel holding a magic wand. Ajaz pulled on the magic wand with both hands. The tunnel gates slowly started to close. He could see a white marble pathway in front of him, and a beautiful lake shore on the other side. Dipping into the lake, the soldier first drank some water, then ate some guavas from a tree there. He plucked a few guavas for his journey and continued walking another six hours before he reached Kadim Shahpur. Ajaz came to my home near sunset, and once he saw me, this soldier Ajaz spoke non-stop for half-an-hour."

Azimuddin continued talking to Mazuddin, whose eyes were already filling with tears. Soon he was weeping uncontrollably. Azimuddin offered the young man a glass of cold water but Mazuddin's tears were falling from his eyes non-stop. Azimuddin thought, "Poor Mazuddin lost his parents both at the same time, and at a young age."

Azimuddin tried to calm Mazuddin down and continued talking, "Your father must have given Ajaz my home address. Look at the wisdom of your father, Mazuddin. In case this soldier who has my home address gets caught while escaping, he has my address, yet your father was willing to risk my life over his son's life. He knew I would not tell anyone where you are, Mazuddin, even if my own life is in danger. I truly and honestly loved your father as my younger brother.

"The fact that he used my five Lessons of life for which he paid me fifty thousand Rupees was enough for me. Your father Aurangzeb definitely won my true love and affection for him. Alas, he is no more."

"Though I am a wealthy businessman, I have no army to defeat a vicious king like Kansa. Instead, I came to the Samajdar boarding school to give you the worst news anyone possibly can give to another person."

Azimuddin continued, "I know the normal reaction would be to take revenge or find and kill King Kansa. Mazuddin, he is guarded around the clock, and is all the more cautious because he knows you are alive. His men are searching for you, day and night. It is only a matter of time before they come here looking for you. You must leave Samajdar boarding school. I have arranged for your departure out of India in a large ship sailing to the city of Bangkok which is located in Thailand. Since the large ship can't get here during the day without getting spotted or noticed by King Kansa's men, it will come late tonight and depart with you."

Mazuddin didn't want to believe his own ears or anything Azimuddin was saying, yet he remembered the respect, admiration, and love his father had for Azimuddin. Mazuddin thought to himself, "If I close my eyes or shut myself in a dark room during daytime hours and say it is night, it will not become night until the sun goes down."

Azimuddin spoke kindly. "Mazuddin, you cannot run away from reality. The truth will always remain a truth, and the truth and reality of your life at this moment is you are a yateem. Your parents are dead, and you are alone in this world."

Mazuddin recognized his own life was in great danger. He'd gone from being a prince to a yateem. The journey had taken less than a half hour. This morning he'd awakened as a prince. He had been sent to Samajdar boarding school to learn about the wisdom of life, and was to return home to become a king of Aurangabad. Instead, tonight he would be sleeping at the beach waiting for the ship to come and pick him up as a yateem.

Azimuddin had given him a bag full of gold coins, saying, "Keep this bag very safely with you at all times, as these coins will help with living expenses. Mazuddin, as a common man, one needs to work to take care of daily living. Since you don't have any such skills, this money will help while you are learning how to survive in this world."

Mazuddin expressed his gratitude first before expressing his dislike for Azimuddin for keeping his father away from him for five years. He remembered his own father had asked him to forgive Azimuddin saying,

"It was my decision to go away without knowing how far and how long I would be away. The time flew by for me. Before I knew it, the five years had passed."

But Mazuddin, from the age of thirteen to eighteen, had waited at the main gate of Aurangabad every day thinking. Today is the day my father will return home.

Azimuddin understood Mazuddin's reasons for resentment and said to Mazuddin, "But that is all in the past now."

The reality was Mazuddin was forced to accept help from the one man he had resented all through his teen years. Yet a part of Mazuddin forgave Azimuddin when his own father asked to be forgiven saying, "It is not Azimuddin's fault, son. It is actually no one's fault. Sometimes life plays its own parts which we are unable to understand. This is why most good and wise people say, "Allah is in control of life. We are not, for Allah works in mysterious ways."

After dinner before leaving Azimuddin said to Mazuddin, "My own wife is very sick with Malaria next few days are very critical for her, so Mazuddin I must leave at once."

Mazuddin expressed his thanks further by saying, "I see why my father loved you so much. You have a sick wife at home and yet you came this far to help me even though I am not your own son."

Mazuddin took a swallow of water and said, "I now banish all dislike for you from my heart, Azimuddin."

Azimuddin was happy to hear this. He said, "Good bye Mazuddin, all the very best with new life in Bangkok."

Azimuddin left.

Wali Sahib called Mazuddin into his own private bedroom. Mazuddin's eyes were still filled with tears. He felt an unfamiliar sadness in his heart, a feeling he hadn't known anything about before now. Wali Sahib sat him down and had his servant bring another glass of cold water.

He said, "Mazuddin, I have had many students here. Some were more intelligent than others. Some learned quickly, some after repeating their mistakes a few times, and some were hopeless so I sent them back within the first three days."

"You, Mazuddin, have been with me for the last five weeks because you are a very good student. You are well-behaved and show a tremendous amount of respect for your teacher and elders. Your listening skills demonstrate how attentive you are. You swim, exercise often, and eat healthy foods that show in your physical appearance."

"You know, Mazuddin, I am able to communicate with angels because I meditated for forty days in a remote forest. This takes utmost discipline and concentration, dedicated devotion and proper recitation from the Holy Quran. Out of a thousand people who try this, only one may succeed. Usually the person gets a slap from the unseen angel that leads to fever which leads to death in a matter of days. Some people die instantly, on the spot. Because of this risk of losing life, very few people try it."

"Since I wanted to find Allah from a young age, I took my chances with life and death, so I am able to communicate with the angels. However, these angels have their own set of rules and guidelines they are required by their creator to follow. They cannot tell you anyone's time or place of birth or death. However, they can show you a way, can give you knowledge of other people's hidden secrets which I am not allowed to misuse in any shape or form."

Wali Sahib drank some water and continued talking, saying, "I am thinking of talking to the angels about you and asking to see if going to Bangkok, in Thailand is the best option for you, Mazuddin, or if there is another option. Ultimately, it's your life we are talking about, so you are the best judge of your decision. Choose what seems most suited for you, Mazuddin."

Mazuddin had always found peace within himself when he walked the lonely beach, especially at sunrise and sunset. Knowing the ship wouldn't come 'til very late at night, Mazuddin asked Wali if he could walk on the beach while waiting. He promised to return in an hour or two.

Wali cautioned Mazuddin. "Be watchful of strangers. If someone asks you any questions say you are working for me as my servant. Avoid any type of suspicion other people might have about you. Be wise. Speak to the point and avoid getting into any long conversations with strangers."

Mazuddin looked a lot like his father. Wali hoped none of Kansa's men would recognize Mazuddin as Aurangzeb's son. This was all Wali could do for now to keep the young prince safe and alive.

While walking, Mazuddin started thinking and talking aloud to himself, knowing he was alone with no one there to hear him. Mazuddin's first thought was, "I am alive today because my father sent me to this Wali's Samajdar boarding school. Surely Kansa would have killed me, too."

Mazuddin remembered he had wanted to stay with his father in his palace, but Aurangzeb had insisted Mazuddin had already learned almost everything there was to learn about palace life. His father had determined it was time for him to go to this school called Samajdar boarding school. It was located in southern Indian, close to Indian ocean and had long stretch of white sandy beach for miles. There he was to meet with a person named Wali Sahib who was spiritually advanced, and had a lot of wisdom and knowledge about our world and the other spiritual world.

Mazuddin was to attend this boarding school for five weeks, to live there and do everything that Mr. Wali Sahib asked of him. He was very well respected in the entire village. People who were his devotees, rich and poor alike, brought Wali Sahib all kinds of gifts. Some brought grains from their harvest; others brought fruits from their plants and gardens, and those who were wealthy business men brought money to put into locked charity boxes.

Wali Sahib was the only one who had the key to this whole place. No guards protected the money boxes that were made of iron. A small slot had been made in each box so people could put their money through it. Wali Sahib used the money for students who came to his boarding school and stayed. Some stayed a short time while others remained for a longer duration, depending on Wali Sahib's evaluation.

There was a sweet-water well built within the walls of the boarding school. Wali Sahib had two servants - one did the cooking. The other helped keep the boarding school clean, tended the garden, and went to the shops to buy milk and whatever else might be needed. Since the boarding school had only ten rooms, Wali Sahib only kept up to five students at a time. Each had his own separate rooms. Even the cook and gardener had their own rooms.

Wali Sahib's real name was Akbar, but everyone called him Wali Sahib. He appeared to be about fifty years old. He'd never married so didn't have any children. He had a full white, well-groomed beard. His partially black mostly grey straight hair was shoulder length. He wore spotless white long Kurta Pajamas, Indian traditional clothes, and brown comfortable-looking leather sandals. Wali had a very distinct look about him which separated him from the rest of the crowd.

Mazuddin was very impressed by Wali Sahib. They'd first met five weeks ago. Every week a new lesson on correct ethical morals or faith was taught, followed by long, meaningful stories which were told, sometimes after breakfast and other times after dinner. Afternoon was usually homework time and personal time for Wali's students.

Students were required to maintain healthy boundaries of mutual respect and care between themselves. Upon his arrival and after his initial introduction to the other four students and cook and gardener, Wali had said to Mazuddin,

"Mazuddin, never disturb me while I am in my private study room as this is the time when I am communicating with my angels, my spiritual world."

And if a student chooses to leave Samajdar boarding school he is free to do so at any given time without explanations.

Wali Sahib believed there is only one final destination. Which road you decide to take there is up to you, but all roads go back to the same destination. Some roads are found in life's junctions. There you are given the choice to pick right or wrong, and every choice has its consequences. The ability to understand right from wrong comes from honorable upbringing by good parents, then good school teachers, then trustworthy associations with good friends and relatives. Wisdom comes from lessons of life.

Wali Sahib was told by his angels "Wali, please share this with your students."

"Allah grant me serenity to accept the things I cannot change, courage to change the things I can and wisdom to know the difference."

Like his father, Mazuddin was very curious by nature, lacked patience, and therefore asked many questions. However, he quickly learned that through being very observant, and just watching others around him, he could absorb much knowledge.

Wali Sahib was quick to put his students in their place. Only three questions were allowed to be asked in the whole day, so students had to think carefully before asking. This reduced unwanted conversations or idle talk which did not lead to productivity. In the last five weeks, Mazuddin had gained much knowledge and wisdom. Walking on the lonesome beach, he reviewed those last five weeks, which seemed in his mind to have passed in the blink of an eye.

Majid's father paused to see if his son was following the story within a story. Satisfied that his son was paying attention, he continued talking.

On Respect

Wali Sahib decided to go to the market and invited Mazuddin and two other students to join him on his visit. At the corner of the market was sitting a fierce-looking local goon who had his gang members working for him. He took money from shop keepers and ate food from their restaurants with his men without paying for it. People gave in to him because they didn't want trouble. Basically, everyone was scared of this goon whose name was Harami. Everyone knew him to be a mean, merciless, shrewd killer who would beat anyone up who did not cooperate with his wishes.

Mazuddin knew nothing of Harami, but two other students who had been with Wali Sahib for a few weeks longer than Mazuddin knew everything about the goon.

As soon as Harami saw Wali Sahib he stood up and said, "As-salamu-alaykum."

Wali Sahib replied, "Wa-Alaikum-As-Salaam."

The greeting the goon had given to Wali Sahib basically meant, "May the peace be upon you."

Wali's reply, "The same to you as well,"

Passed between them in Arabic.

Junaid, one of wali's students who understood the language, was explaining the meaning to the other students. The exchange finished, they picked up fruits and vegetables and chicken cut Halal, the Kosher way that had been cleaned and cut to small pieces. The food was put in a bag made of coconut leaves and brought back to the ashram for cooking.

As they were headed toward the boarding school Junaid, who knew about the three questions rule nevertheless asked Wali Sahib, "Why do you reply to the goon's salaam, Wali Sahib? Everyone knows he is a bad guy, so why maintain any association with such a bad person?"

This was one question with two parts. Wali Sahib didn't bother to reply anything to Junaid, who knew not to demand an answer from his teacher.

That night before going to sleep Mazuddin asked Junaid about Harami. After hearing his long rap sheet of wrong doings, Mazuddin agreed with Junaid that Wali Sahib should not maintain any relationship with such a bad guy. Why Wali Sahib did the things he did, and the way he did them, was best known only by Wali Sahib.

After breakfast the next day, Wali Sahib decided to go back to the market, this time to buy some goat meat. He asked Mazuddin, Junaid, and Javed to come along. The other two students who were a few years younger than these, and not as bright stayed at the boarding school. They needed to study more and do more homework to catch up with the older boys.

Once again, when they reached the market Harami was sitting at his usual spot, his back toward Wali Sahib, so didn't see him coming. Otherwise, he would have stood up and said, "Salaam."

About twenty steps away from the goon Wali Sahib turned to Junaid and said, "Junaid, go slap Harami as hard as you can."

Junaid looked at Wali Sahib in shock, wondering if he'd heard his teacher correctly.

"You want me to slap the goon as hard as I can?"

Wali Sahib said, "Yes."

Junaid thought, "This is the end of me. The goon will surely kill me."

Yet he could not disobey an order given by Wali Sahib. That was the first requirement for becoming and remaining Wali Sahib's student.

Wali Sahib had said, "No student should ever disobey my direct orders and commands."

Junaid walk slowly, hesitantly toward the goon while Wali Sahib, Mazuddin and Javed stood watching a few steps away and behind the goon who was sitting there counting his money. Junaid took advantage of the situation when Harami, who was not looking around, and slapped him as hard as he could. The goon was in complete astonishment. Who had the courage to slap him? He reacted instinctively. He looked at this young boy, barely eighteen years of age, standing there staring at him with frightened eyes. The goon got up, took out his dagger and, just before striking the boy, realized he was a student of Wali Sahib. He remembered seeing him with Wali Sahib. He looked into the eyes of the boy named Junaid and said,

"I am going to spare your life only because you are a student of Wali Sahib, and I have utmost respect for him. Get away from me at once."

As Junaid walked back toward his teacher, Harami turned to see Wali Sahib was standing there. The goon, in his polite tone, once again said to Wali Sahib,

"Please keep your students away from me for their sake. No one dares slap me."

Wali Sahib apologized to Harami and said, "I was trying to teach a lesson to my students which required slapping you. It will never happen again."

In a very calm tone goon said, "In that case, I will consider it never happened."

They said good-bye to each other. Wali Sahib and his students picked up their halal goat meat and returned to Samajdar boarding school. After lunch Wali Sahib sat all three students down and asked, "What did you learn from our visit to the market today?"

Junaid, who was still in complete shock, had not uttered a word since slapping the goon. Javed wanted to reply but Wali Sahib raised his hand up and gestured him to keep quiet while he asked Mazuddin to reply to his question.

Mazuddin responded, "You had started this week's lesson on Respect. I had not known anything about Harami until Junaid explained the circumstances to me last night. I was wondering about the same thing as Junaid. Why associate with a famous goon? However, after seeing today's incident in the market, I totally understand the concept of respect. If someone respects you for being a famous good guy and decides to show his respect by offering to say 'Salaam' to you first, you must respond back with the same respect. Treat others the way you want to be treated. Respect is supposed to be a two-way street, not a one-way. It is only the respect Harami has for you that spared the life of Junaid. Otherwise, he was ready to kill Junaid with his dagger."

Wali Sahib said, "Well said. Good answer Mazuddin."

And Junaid, who was completely silent all this time, looked at Wali Sahib and said, "I am extremely sorry. Please forgive me for thinking you should not associate with a famous goon like Harami. I have learned my lesson on respect, Wali Sahib."

Their homework assignment for the remainder of the week was to go outside of the boarding school and do kind acts with complete strangers, and gain their respect, liking, and trust. All three students of Wali Sahib followed their assignment. Mazuddin, being strong, liked to work outside. He picked up a community service job as water filler from the well of the village. He also picked up pot after pot and decided to bring water to everybody's homes. Pregnant women with young children, along with their older parents, thanked Mazuddin.

Junaid offered a free house-cleaning service for many homes near the boarding school. Javed was fond of baking, so he baked sweets for many families living close to the boarding school. And as expected, many home owners and their families around the boarding school got acquainted with Mazuddin, Javed, and Junaid, and their respect for these three young men grew.

Majid's father said to Majid, "You see, son, earning respect can be far more useful than anything else at times."

Majid nodded his head and said, "Yes, Abbu Ji. I will live to earn respect in my life."

His father continued talking to Majid.

Greed is not good. Be satisfied.

Wali Sahib started the story at breakfast time and continued nearly until noon when lunch was ready to be served. Wali spoke to his students in his calm tone and continued, telling yet another story.

"Once upon a time in a faraway village lived a poor farmer with his old parents. He was their only son and his name was Hasan. At a young age Hasan started helping his father in farming work and learned to be a good farmer himself. As his father grew old, Hasan was turning into a young man. He told his daddy he would take over all the work on the farm, and asked his daddy to stay home and look after his mother. From time to time, he turned to his daddy for suggestions and advice.

The months turned into years, and when Hasan was twenty-one years old, his father started looking for a woman for Hasan to marry.

And his mother said to him, "Hasan, I am growing old along with your father. Find a woman to marry you. She will look after us, cook for us, keep the home clean, and give us healthy grandchildren."

Hasan thought, "I am still young and cannot find any woman attractive enough to be my wife."

His father's suggestion of marrying the daughter of one of his friends fell on Hasan's deaf ears.

Hasan stated flatly to his old parents, "I don't find her attractive enough to be my wife."

After pressuring their son to get married for the next two to three years, his parents decided to leave the whole "Hasan's marriage" subject alone.

Once every year a Fun & Fair event was held in the expansive open-wide grounds close to a few villages. Many people came there for entertainment.

Some liked to ride on a big merry-go-round or windmill, while others watched magic shows. This fair was called a Mela. It was the place where everyone seemed to forget the worries of their daily lives. During their visit inside the Mela, they were happy and joyful.

Hasan decided to take his old parents to this Mela. He arranged to borrow two donkeys for his parents to ride on. Because of their old age, walking long distances was not an option for them. The journey was not too long, and his parents were happy to see the sights and chat with old friends.

Hasan had finished a good lunch with his parents and was preparing to go into a tent to watch a magic show when he suddenly noticed the woman of his dreams. She was tall and slender with straight long black hair and a very attractive pretty face with dark brown eyes. She noticed Hasan, too. All the years of being a farmer and doing hard work in the fields had given Hasan a well-built body, and he himself was a very good-looking man - poor but good-looking.

Hasan instantly showed this girl to his parents just as the girl was showing Hasan to her two young female friends when his father looked closely at one of the three girls.

Hasan's father said to Hasan, "You refused to marry her a few years ago."

Hasan replied, "That one I recognize myself Daddy. I am talking about the tall slender one with long black hair. She is wearing a light pink dress, and she is girl I would like to marry. She is more than attractive-looking. She is a very beautiful girl, Daddy."

His daddy looked closely and noticed her then.

He said, "She looks very pretty son. Her name is Hasina, if my memory serves me right. She is the only daughter of a rich merchant, and little bit spoiled with an overdose of love and money. She is their only daughter so her parents do everything she wants. I have heard she has a short temper and has refused many marriage proposals from other wealthy families. Because we are poor she may never want to marry you Hasan."

While Hasan and his father were talking, the attractive girl whose name was Hasina was asking her friend Salma, "Salma do you know who this handsome man is?"

Salma replied, "I know about him. Two years ago he refused my marriage proposal. His name is Hasan, and he is a poor farmer."

Hasina didn't pay attention to the last part of her friend's sentence as she found Hasan very handsome and attractive and thought. This is the man I want to marry.

At the same time, Hasan's father was saying to Hasan, "I will go speak to the merchant and ask for his daughter's hand in marriage to you."

Hasan and Hasina looked at each other for a few more seconds before other people started walking in front of them. The magic show was about to begin so Hasan had to go inside the tent.

The next day, Hasan's father left on his donkey to go to merchant's home which was very big and lavish-looking from the outside. Hasan's father Awal rang the bell outside the main door. A servant opened the door and asked, "Who are you looking for, sir?"

And Awal replied, "My name is Awal. I am here to talk to Hasina's father if he is home."

The servant left the door ajar and went to call Hasina's father. Standing there at the door Awal noticed the inside of this home was even better than the outside. Expensive rugs were spread on the floors. Paintings adorned the walls, and good wooden furniture tastefully decorated the room.

Awal heard the servant call out, "Mr. Aziz, there is someone here at door to see you."

Aziz came out of his study room where he was busy doing accounting for his business. He was very well dressed, a distinguished-looking man.

He looked at the poor farmer and thought. Another one has come looking for free money or a handout of some sort. Being wealthy can be a curse at times. People are always asking for something.

So he asked, "Who are you and what do you want with me?"

The wealthy merchant now remembered seeing Hasan's father working his farm land, while Aziz went to college to get a better education.

Awal knew the merchant's tone of voice all too well. As a poor farmer, he had heard it before and said, "Despite not wanting to come to your door, my son whom I love very much requested I come to your door. He likes your daughter, he saw your daughter for the first time at the Mela yesterday, and my son wishes to marry your daughter."

The rich merchant almost shouted, "Are you out of your mind, you poor old farmer? Has anyone taught you the saying, 'Birds of a feather flock together?'"

Aziz was almost ready to dismiss the poor farmer and shut the door on his face, while his daughter, who had just finished taking a shower, was trying to figure out what to wear, as her wardrobe was filled with clothes. Hasina heard the conversation her daddy was having at the main door of their home. Thinking this could be the father of her handsome, attractive husband-to-be, she hurriedly put on a gown and came running to see who was talking to her father. Hasina saw the poor old farmer at the door and instantly remembered seeing him with his handsome son.

Right away she said to her father, Aziz, "Daddy, I like this poor farmer's handsome son. I wish to marry him as well."

Aziz turned to his rich spoiled daughter and replied, "Hasina, they are very poor farmers. They will not able to offer you comfortable beds to sleep on. Their entire home is no larger than my study room alone. They won't be able to provide you with the tasty lavish foods that you are used to eating and they don't have servants because they are too poor to pay any servant to work for them."

But Hasina, being stubborn from childhood and always getting whatever she wanted, didn't pay much attention to her father's advice or suggestions. She insisted she had decided she wanted to be the wife of a poor but very handsome man.

The next week the wedding took place. It was an odd mix of rich and poor. The merchant's friends and relatives were rich and came in their horse-driven carriage, whereas the farmer's friends and relatives mostly came walking or on donkeys, wearing mediocre clothes.

The merchant had arranged for a lavish dinner and extravagant wedding celebration of fireworks. After the elaborate wedding reception, a horse-driven carriage was sent to the poor farmer's home with Hasina and Hasan in it.

Within days of her marriage, Hasina started ill-treating Hasan's parents. She spoke to them with disrespect, but because Hasan stayed outside on the farm all day long, he didn't know how Hasina was treating his parents.

The poor parents of Hasan didn't want to hurt their son's feelings. After all, he loved Hasina very much, so they kept quiet about Hasina's ill-treatment towards them. Hasina was forcing Hasan's old parents to wait on her and cook for her and wash clothes for her, basically treating them like servants. This took its toll on Hasan's old parents. First, it was Hasan's father who got sick from pneumonia and died because he lacked proper medication. Due to poverty, Hasan couldn't buy expensive medicines. He cried at the loss of his father, but being a poor farmer, he had to return to work in his farm the very next day.

This did not affect Hasina at all. In fact, now Hasan's mother had to work twice as much. She missed her husband and when alone and away from Hasina, she often cried. Meanwhile, Hasan was away working in his farm. His old mother was overworked and heartbroken due to her husband's death. The extra work took its toll on her.

She was at the well washing one of Hasina's expensive dress in the peak of the afternoon sun. Hasina had insisted she needed to wear that dress to her friend's home that evening. The poor old woman died of a heart attack right next to the well by their home. When Hasina needed to eat her lunch, she started calling out to Hasan's mother who was not answering back. This lazy old woman. It takes her two hours just to wash one of my dress.

In a rage, she went looking for the old woman only to find her dead body lying by the well. Hasina removed her dress from the well, rinsed it herself with fresh water, and hung it out to dry out.

Hasina was not affected at all by the old woman's death. She went to get Hasan to tell him lies. "I had told your mother not to go to the well as I would get the water for home in the evening when sun is not so hot, but your mother paid no heed to my advice or suggestion, and look how hot sun got to her."

Hasan, who loved his wife very much, thought, perhaps his mother had died because she hadn't listened to his wife. Hasan cried again at the loss of his loving mother.

He thought to himself. Both my parents grew old and died. Perhaps they are in a better place with Allah.

Hasina asked him to take rest of the day off to take care of the funeral. "Stay at home today and cook dinner for me."

Hasan quickly learned that Hasina didn't know how to cook or clean the house, and he decided to hire a servant to clean the home for her. Instead of eating three meals a day he cut down on his lunch. He ate dry bread with raw onions to save money to pay for the servant.

Hasina's demands for better material things never seemed to end. Hasan was trying to offer his wife the life of a millionaire on a poor working farmer's budget. But somehow Hasan felt Hasina loved him. Why else would she stay with a poor farmer like him? It was his fault that he didn't go to school or college to get a better education. Then he could have gotten a better job and been able to offer a better life to someone like Hasina whom he loved very much.

Hasina always went to see her parents for her good clothes and shoes. She even asked for money at times for herself. Since Hasina's parents were used to throwing money on their only daughter, they didn't mind it at all.

Hasan noticed all this and one day he said to his wife, "Sweetheart, now you are a married woman, my wife. I don't like that you go to your parents for clothes, shoes, jewelry, and even spending money so you can continue to spend money around your friends."

Hasina bluntly replied, "Hasan, I am used to doing whatever I want. If you don't like me asking my own parents for money, why don't you figure out how to get me the good quality clothes, shoes, Jewelry, and spending money I need when I am around my friends?"

It was a slap in Hasan's face. He knew he could never buy these types of expensive clothes or shoes for his wife. The dresses and shoes she wore were costlier than the money he earned in an entire month of working very hard in his farm.

He thought to himself. Some things you can change, and some things are better left alone.

Hasina knew Hasan to be a good farmer and was constantly trying to figure out how she could get her husband to make more money.

One late afternoon Hasina was getting bored and hungry at home, so decided to hang out in the farm with her husband. As she was approaching Hasan, she noticed he was sitting and eating dry bread with some onions, resting his back against a big old dried-out tree. A few big boulders rose up here and there, but land itself looked barren. Hasan saw his wife coming toward him so he smiled and started to get up, but Hasina said,

"No. Sit down and eat your food. I was getting bored at home so decided to come visit you."

Hasan was happy to see his wife and thought to himself, "She must love me. Why else she would walk all this way to my farm?"

Hasina asked Hasan, "Is this land where you are sitting ours or does it belong to other farmers?"

Hasan replied, "It belongs to us. We have thirty acres of land."

And he showed her the boundaries of his land.

This is when Hasina said, "You are a very good farmer. I have noticed that about you."

Hasan smiled again and thought to himself. Today must be a special day.

He had never known his wife to compliment him on anything.

Next Hasina said, "This tree where you are sitting is dead. It does not provide much shade. There is no question of flowers or fruits, and these boulders don't do much for you either."

Hasan was thinking and wondering. Where is she going with all this?

But he waited patiently for Hasina to finish talking before he asked any questions.

Hasina continued, "IF you cut this tree down, dig up some land around it, and take out the dead tree roots, you can create more farm land. How about taking these boulders out? I know they are large, but you can break them down into small pieces with hammer, one boulder at a time. Soon they all will be gone and you will have all this extra land to farm on. Perhaps we can grow some mango trees here. They take five years to give their first fruit, but mangos sell well and for a very good price, and I love eating mangos myself."

And Hasan thought to himself. So this what it was all about – ultimately, more money.

He knew the cost on him the labor would be. His wife had no clue how much hard work it would be for him. She knew nothing about how difficult it is to break down big boulders. There were several of them in this patch of his land. Hasina was looking at Hasan with eager eyes for an answer.

Hasan, who liked pleasing his wife at all cost said, "I will start it tomorrow as soon as I have a chance after cultivating the other side of our farm."

Hasina said, "It is almost four o'clock. Let's go home together. I am feeling hungry. You need to cook some food for me. I have been to the market and purchased some goat meat, your favorite."

Hasan once again thought, So, she came by not because she was really bored or was missing me. She was hungry and not knowing how to cook, came looking for her husband to cook an early dinner for her.

Hasan picked up his farming tools and put them in a shed next to the barn, then joined his wife on the long walk back to their home. Fortunately, Hasan was a good cook. His mother had taught him how to cook and he had learned well from her.

After eating a good dinner, Hasan went to the well outside their home, fetched two buckets of water, took a refreshing shower, and was ready to go to bed. Hasina had taken her shower while Hasan was busy cooking dinner. As Hasan walked inside the dimly lit bedroom there was a big surprise waiting for him. His wife was completely naked, and lying in bed waiting for him. It was usually the other way around. Hasan would have to request his wife to make love to him and she would usually turn him down, giving one excuse or the other.

"I don't feel like it today. Maybe tomorrow."

And sometimes it would be a week before that tomorrow even came. Yes, after almost two years of marriage with Hasina, this was definitely different for him. Hasan welcomed the change with a bright smile on his face and joy in his heart.

They made love and went to sleep in each other's arms. Hasan's last thought before falling asleep was so this is what it feels like to be happily married and in love with your wife.

Early the next morning Hasan got up and went into his backyard looking for an axe to cut that old tree down. The axe hadn't been used for a long time and needed to replaced, but a new axe would be expensive. The old one would have to do for now. He also picked up the biggest hammer he had in his backyard. It had been given to his father as a gift by his friend who was an iron smith by trade.

Hasan was already in the habit of making breakfast and lunch sandwiches for his wife every day before leaving for work in his farm. Cooking for her daily had become a habit.

Since he didn't have any help like some other farmers did, he has an enormous amount of work to finish each day. Hiring help would mean less money for his wife. So he moved as quickly as he could, eating his light breakfast quickly while working. For lunch, he ate dry bread and onion again while working.

Around 5pm when he was finished with his regular farming, he headed toward the big tree, thinking this big tree used to be my resting spot. I enjoyed resting my back against its rough bark. Now this tree has to go away because Hasina wants me to farm this portion of the land as well for her mango trees.

He almost said aloud to himself, knowing no one is around to listen, "Look at the bright side of the picture Hasan. In next five to eight years this place will be covered with mango trees. They will provide shade, and fruits to eat and sell. Mango tree trunks get larger at the base as they grow older. Then I can use it to rest my back against."

As he visualized this portion of his land with lush green mango trees, he felt better. He picked up his axe and was ready to take his first swing, but before he could strike the tree, a male voice spoke from it:

"Stop! Don't cut down this tree."

Hasan was shocked and surprised at the same time. He knew there was no one around, so he frantically started looking to see if someone was hiding behind the dead old dry tree.

This is when he heard the voice again, definitely a male voice that said, "Hasan, I have been living inside this tree for too many years now. If you cut down this tree I will lose my home. Please don't cut it down and take away my home."

At this point Hasan knew he was not hallucinating. He was not day-dreaming. There was indeed a person talking from inside the tree.

Hasan said, "Show me yourself."

Instantly a male Angel dressed in a white robe and with wings on each of his shoulders. Radiant face shining, he came out of the tree and said, "If you don't cut this tree I will grant you one wish which will come true."

Hasan was amazed at what was happening in front of his very eyes. He thought long and hard, then quickly, and thought again, "What should I ask for? If I ask for gold, my wife may say, 'Why didn't you ask for diamonds as they are more valuable money wise?' He could not decide what to ask for as he was too scared of displeasing his wife.

The Angel, who was waiting patiently spoke again, "Wish for what you want Hasan."

Hasan replied to the Angel, "You see, I love my wife very much and am afraid of displeasing her. May I consult her before I make my decision?"

The Angel responded. "I will be waiting to hear your wife's wish. Go talk to her and return with your wish."

Hasan threw his hammer and axe in his farm shed and came running to see his wife. Hasan remembered Hasina had gone to visit her friends. He knew that every Sunday she went to meet with her friends. Sometimes she came home late as she and her friends would go out and have their fancy dinner in some well-reputed good restaurant. Many times Hasina brought home leftovers. Sometimes she brought a very fine dinner for Hasan, too.

Hasan managed to keep himself busy but somehow tonight was different. There was an urgent question he needed Hasina's answer to, and it bothered him that his wife was so late in coming home. He needed her to help him with his one wish which indirectly would be her wish.

Hasan fixed himself a chicken sandwich and waited patiently for his wife. As time ticked away, he was tempted to make the wish without consulting her, but he had always worked on pleasing his wife and this "ONE WISH" was a big decision that Hasan didn't want to take alone. He started pacing back and forth in front of his home.

Finally, little after 9pm, Hasina came home. Her friends dropped her in their horse-driven carriage and Hasina, who was used to finding her husband fast asleep in bed, was surprised to see him pacing outside their home. Hasan watched Hasina's friends saying good-bye before turning their carriage and starting away.

Hasan called out to Hasina, "Hasina, my dear wife, I have something very important to tell you."

Hasina, who treated her husband as a very ordinary farmer said, "Whatever it is you wish to tell me has to wait as I have to rush to the toilet first."

Again Hasan waited for his wife to finish using the toilet, which seemed to Hasan like an eternity. Finally, when Hasina came out Hasan was waiting right outside the door for her.

He held Hasina's hand and led her into their living room. They sat down together on a wooden sofa that Hasan himself had made for Hasina.

She was a bit amazed at Hasan's urgency but decided to hear him out, wondering. What is so important that my husband has to tell me?

Hasan said, "There is a male angel in the tree"

Hasina asked, "What tree? "

Hasan explained, "The tree you asked me to cut down, that big dry old tree by all those boulders on our farm."

It took a moment for Hasina to recollect that she had asked him to chop down the big dry dead old tree and grow mango trees instead. Not believing what her husband was trying to say Hasina responded, "Hasan, you are making up stories because you don't want to cut down that tree. I remember your telling me how you like to rest your back against it.

"Don't be lazy, Hasan. Imagine how those mango trees will provide rest for your back, shade for your face, and fruits to eat and sell."

She continued by saying, "If you don't want to do this, then I will be forced to ask my daddy for help. I am sure he will give me enough money to hire workers to make my mango farm idea come true."

Hasan looked at Hasina, complete hopefulness in his face. Again he spoke. "Hasina, if you don't believe me why don't you come with me at once and see this radiant male angel. He even has wings on either side of his back shoulders."

Hasina was about to slap Hasan, but controlled herself. She went and helped herself to a glass of water to calm herself down because what her husband was saying didn't make any sense. There are no angels that live in trees.

Hasan had already offered to take Hasina to see the angel. Hasina knew Hasan had never lied to her about anything, and also knew he truly loved her.

Drinking the water helped her think better, and she said, "It is late but I want that tree cut down first thing in the morning so let's go now; let's look at your imaginary male angel with wings and a radiant face."

It was almost 10pm by the time they reached the big old dry tree. Hasan called out, "Angel, Angel please wake up. I have brought my wife with me to see you because she does not believe that you actually live in this tree."

Hasina, who was standing right next to the big old dry tree with Hasan, started thinking and wondering at the same time. Has my husband gone completely insane, bananas, cuckoo in the head? Has the hot summer sun fried his brains? He is actually talking to a tree.

The longer it took for her husband's imaginary angel to respond the more convinced Hasina was that her husband had lost it in the head. Hasan desperately needed the angel to answer his call. He didn't want Hasina to think he was lying or crazy in the head, so he called out again, this time much more loudly.

"Angel, please come and show yourself to my wife. Otherwise, she will think I am lying and have gone nuts in my head. Angel, please come out."

He was screaming so loudly Hasina was sure at least a few farmers in nearby areas heard Hasan screaming at the dead tree.

As Hasina was ready to take Hasan away from the tree and ridicule him, the angel appeared. Though it was pitch dark at this time of the night, it was as if someone had turned on a light. Light was shining from the angel's whole glowing body through his long white loose clothes.

Hasina thought. Now I see what Hasan meant by a radiant face. It was indeed a male angel with wings, wearing a white long robe. The angel was hovering in the air as earth's gravity didn't affect him.

The angel said, "I was busy praying. I had to take a break during my prayers to show myself to you Hasina because you disbelieve your own husband."

Hasina was speechless, just stunned. She stood there like a statue, and the angel spoke again, "Have you decided, Hasan, what to wish for? Remember, I do have to get back to my prayers."

This time Hasina brought herself to her senses, and spoke on behalf of Hasan, who was waiting for her to say something to the angel.

Hasina said to him, "Can we think for a moment? After all, it is only one wish. Even fairy tales have three to seven wishes. May we think about our single, solitary, one and only wish?"

The angel wasn't pleased that Hasina was comparing one wish with many wishes of fairy tales, but decided to ignore it. He said, "I say my prayers all night long, and do not wish to be disturbed again. Hence, think about your one wish and return to me at sunrise. Ask what you wish for and I shall grant it."

Hasan and Hasina walked back to their home silently, each doing their own thinking. Hasina thought. Good fortune finally came knocking at my door. Only because I thought of the mango farm, all this is happening. Now the biggest question is what one wish to ask for.

Hasina thought about asking for gold, which can be stolen. Diamonds can be stolen, too. How was she to become rich and remain rich without fearing loss of the wealth?

Then Hasan asked Hasina, "What are you thinking?"

She decided to bring him into her thinking process. Though she treated her husband as a dumb bird, she decided to share her ideas with Hasan, and said, "Gold and diamonds can be stolen. That will make us poor again. How to become rich and remain rich is what I am thinking about."

Hasan took pride in knowing he married a very beautiful and smart woman, a bit demanding at times but smart. However, it was Hasan who came up with the idea about asking for more land to farm on.

Hasan said to Hasina, "I am a good farmer. If I have more land I can farm more. We will become rich and remain rich, as it will be my land. No one can steal my land. Gold and diamonds can be stolen by thieves."

Hasina liked the idea, and thought to herself. He is not such a dumb bird after all.

They had decided to ask for more farm land. Now the question became how to ask for more land, which village, what direction of land they wished to be theirs. Both husband and wife thought for another two hours before giving up. They decided to ask for a suggestion from the male angel, and if his suggestion sounded good, they would act on it.

Hasan and Hasina were so excited they only slept for two hours from 4am to 6am so they could make it to the tree before sunrise. As expected, on the first ray of sun light the angel appeared and asked, "Have you made up your mind about that "one wish" of yours?"

Hasina spoke. "We have decided to get more farm land. Hasan is a good farmer and knows all about farming. We do not wish for gold or diamonds as they can be stolen and we would be back to being poor."

The Angel liked this woman's cunning thinking, and asked, "How will you decide how much land to get, and in which direction to go?"

Hasina said, "Because we could not decide we came to you to help us decide."

The angel spoke again. "Why don't you pick a direction and walk or run in that direction from the first rays of sun light to the last ray of sunset. Whatever land Hasan covers will belong to him. Use no horses or donkeys, no carriages either. Because this is going to be his land, he needs to step on it, tell the earth, the ground beneath his feet to know their new owner. Since the sun is already quite high, we will start this tomorrow morning at sunrise. Go enjoy your day together as Husband and Wife."

Hasan and his wife Hasina ate their breakfast and decided to get a little bit of sleep.

Hasina said to Hasan, "Tired minds don't think well. We must sleep for a few hours and get up by afternoon. Then we can debate which direction to pick."

Hasan enjoyed his day off from farming, and they both woke up late in the afternoon. Hasan made lunch for both of them. Once finished eating their meal, they started their thinking process again. Time was ticking by, and yet neither of them could come up with a good direction to pick. Before they knew it, the sun was setting.

They ate the dinner Hasan had prepared, then husband and wife stayed up 'til the wee hours of the night, debating which direction Hasan should run.

It was decided that in order to cover more land, Hasan must run as fast as he could. Hasina, who had travelled a little bit more than Hasan, knew the northeast direction had a river going through the land toward the sea, which was still four villages away. If Hasan could cross that river before sunset, Hasan and Hasina would be set for life. Hasina was smart and knew farmers suffer the most in the years that do not see much rain, whereas if the river runs through your land, you can get all the water you need for farming. She knew this "Krishna river" never runs dry. It originates from spring waters from the mountains to the north, so the direction was chosen. It was decided Hasan was to run. He was also supposed to carry a sack of water made out of leather.

Hasina said, "Keep drinking water while running. This will keep you hydrated."

They decided Hasan was to drink lots of water. He found a good comfortable pair of shoes that his father used to wear for special occasions. They looked almost brand new. Hasan didn't want to ruin a good pair of his father's shoes by wearing them in the muddy waters of his farm. He had saved these shoes, hoping to wear them if a special occasion arose. There can't be a better time to wear these shoes than today. Yes, I will wear my father's shoes.

By the time all these decisions had been made it was already 3am. Hasan kept waking up every half hour or so because he didn't want to accidentally fall into a deep sleep and miss his appointment with the angel who was going to grant him his one wish.

Hasan woke at 5:30am. He decided to get out of bed and get ready for the day. He gazed at his beautiful wife who was fast asleep. Hasan was feeling very tired and sleepy. He had not slept well these past two nights, but had to get up early for his wife's one wish.

Hasan took a cold water shower hoping it would refresh him, which it did. He ate his breakfast quickly, and made breakfast and a sandwich for lunch. Not sure at what time he would get home, and knowing his wife loves spinach and chicken, he prepared a delicious dinner for his wife and left a note at her dinner plate which read:

"I LOVE YOU VERY MUCH HASINA. YOU ARE THE LOVE OF MY LIFE, MY WIFE. ENJOY YOUR DINNER AS I DON'T KNOW WHEN WILL I RETURN."

Love Hasan.

Hasan was at the tree fifteen minutes before sunrise. The sky shimmered in the clear dawn light. High above, birds were soaring and flying. Hasan noticed some pretty butterflies flying around, too.

He thought to himself. Summer is such a good time of the year. Everything comes to life. If only it didn't get so hot during the day, it would be perfect.

Yet this morning looked extra special to Hasan because he was about to become the richest, wealthiest landlord that had ever lived. He made elaborate plans in his mind about hiring hundreds of farmers like himself who would plow his land. He would buy sheep and cows and goats, open a farm house as well. The sky was no limit to Hasan's success.

6:15am: He was still lost in deep thought when he heard the angel's voice saying, "Hasan. Are you ready?"

Hasan shook himself out of his day dreaming and replied, "Yes angel, I am ready."

As he spoke, the sun's first rays of light started shining onto Hasan's face. He was supposed to run in the direction of the sunrise, northeast, so Hasan started running. The water sack tied to Hasan's waist constantly jumped and bounced. Within minutes it started to pound so hard against Hasan's waist it hurt. He took it off and held it with both hands, as it was too heavy to be carried with one hand. Hasina had made sure she gave him a very big sack of water. Hasan noticed because of this water sack he was unable to run fast.

Following considerable thought, Hasan made a decision. I can hide this sack behind a mango tree belonging to my wealthy neighboring farmer. Upon my return, I will drink more water from it and throw the rest away. Hasina will never know if I drank the water or threw it away. This heavy sack is her idea and it is slowing me down.

So Hasan put the water sack behind the mango tree and started running again. This time Hasan was able to run fast as the wind. He didn't know he was capable of running so fast. Within an hour of running, Hasan had left his own village behind. Entering the next village, he looked up and saw the sun was already getting high. Constantly looking in the direction of the rising sun was hurting Hasan's eyes, but that was the direction he was running toward.

Hasan had to keep an eye on approaching rocks or puddle of waters. Avoiding them so he didn't fall and hurt himself was proving to be bit difficult.

Hasan thought if I slow down it may be easier to avoid the rocks while I am running, but then I won't be able to cross the river. Hasina wants me to cross the river.

Hasan kept running as fast as he could.

8:00am: It was 8am already. Hasan had started running at 6:15am. He'd been running very fast non-stop for almost two hours and he was already leaving the second village behind. Hasan remembered his wife had said, "This river comes after the fourth village."

So Hasan was feeling happy about his progress.

9:00am: Hasan kept running. By the time he was entering the third village, he was feeling very thirsty. The physical exertion from non-stop running for the past three hours was tiring. This third village had lots of hills, some small, some large.

Running up was proving to be physically challenging. Running down from a hill seemed even harder because Hasan would pick up so much speed he had to use all his strength to slow himself down. He did the best he could, and kept running up and down.

It was almost 10am and this village with endless hills did not seem to end. Hasan thought this must be the biggest village around because he has been running in it for almost over an hour.

While running, Hasan kept thinking how impossible his wife's demands were for her "wish" or "suggestion" to have him cross the river after the fourth village. He was still stuck in the third village with its endless hills. Hasan was finding it harder and harder to climb the hills. When he could no longer run up the hill he started walking as fast as he could. Going down the hill, he managed to run.

11:00am It was close to 11am. The sun was no longer shining in his eyes but shining over his head. It was a warm summer day in south India where temperatures go up to 40 degrees Celsius, 104 Fahrenheit. Hasan was feeling every bit of the heat. He was sweating buckets of perspiration. His T-Shirt had been soaked with sweat for the past three hours.

When Hasan walked up yet another hill, it seemed much taller than the hills he had climbed earlier in the day. It took Hasan almost an hour just to get to the top of this hill. Once on top of this tallest hill, he looked out on this clear sunny day. He could see far into the distance. Sunlight was dancing on a body of water which looked to Hasan like a river. The sunlight on the river dazzled his eyes. The shimmering sunlight on the river looked breathtakingly beautiful.

Hasan smiled for a moment and thought. Here is where I will build my new home so I can look at this beautiful view any time. This will all be my land. At last I can see the river, so the fourth village must be between here and that river.

Hasan hoped the fourth village would not be as big as this one, with its endless hills. Looking into the distance, he could see there were five more hills to cross. Beyond them, the land looked more flat. Hasan was feeling so thirsty that his mouth was completely dry. He thought perhaps the next village would have a well where he could drink some water.

11:45am: Hasan was climbing his last hill. On the other side of this hill the land was flat. Soon he'd reach his river. It was taking every ounce of energy in Hasan to climb up this final hill. He was doing this to prove his love for his beautiful wife. Hasan reached the top of this hill and suddenly felt enormous pain in his chest. His lungs were begging for more oxygen; he was already huffing and puffing. He had been breathing heavily for over five-and-a-half hours. Exertion from all this running was finally showing its effects.

Hasan felt light-headed and fell down. He was experiencing cardiac arrest, the abrupt cessation of his heart beat, and within moments Hasan's heart gave out. His heart completely stopped, and he died there on top of his last hill.

As Angel AZRAEL was taking the soul of Hasan with him, he asked the radiant male angel who lived in the tree, "Why did you kill the poor farmer? He was living happily, fulfilling the wishes of his wife whom he loved so much."

Wali paused to take a sip of water and looked at his students paying good attention to his story, he continued talking to his students, saying, "Angels can talk and see each other at any given moment of time. Free of the boundaries of our world, their abilities are beyond our comprehension."

The Radiant male angel replied, "Hasan's greed killed him, not me. Look at Hasan lying dead there. How much land did he really need? How much land does he really need to be buried? Perhaps a maximum of eight feet long by four feet wide and six feet deep. How much land does any human need to be buried in? This is his everlasting resting place. It's all the land he needs. Yet Hasan ran and ran in the hope of becoming the wealthiest landlord that ever lived.

"In order to please his ever-demanding wife, Hasan ran himself to his own death. If only these humans would acknowledge, understand, and respect the facts of their humanly lives. They come empty-handed from their mother's womb, and when they die, they go empty-handed to their grave. They cannot take their big homes, and the big lands they wish to own and farm to their grave. Their expensive belongings, their big castles, diamond studded gold crowns, are left behind, along with all of this world's wealth. These riches do not go to their grave with them. What they make here stays here.

What does go with them is how they lived on this beautiful Earth, made by Allah, how many times they understood the difference between right and wrong and did the right thing or acted rightly even though that seemed far more difficult to do then doing the wrong thing. If only these humans understood. Allah has not been partial with them. He gave them one heart, one brain. The blood color in all humans is red, yet they feel the need to be partial with each other.

Islamic Muslim people believe there are angels sitting on both their shoulders. When they do something right, the angel on their right shoulder writes it down. When they do something wrong, the angel on the left shoulder writes it down. Twenty-four hours a day, seven days a week, and at all times of their lives, when a Muslim person who believes in Islam dies, these angels from each shoulder present to Allah the details of right versus wrong, correct versus incorrect, good versus evil. Then Allah decides if they go to heaven or hell.

Greed is not a good quality to have. Greed is considered evil, yet our human race has this all-consuming greed that never seems to be fulfilled or satisfied. Look at our poor little farmer. His greed was so large that he wanted to run across four villages and reach the river so he could become the wealthiest landlord of this world. He died trying to fulfill that greed."

The Radiant male angel continued saying to AZRAEL, "Take his soul to Allah and let Allah be the judge of heaven or hell for his soul."

AZRAEL said to the Radiant angel, "As we both know Allah is most kind, most merciful, most forgiving. Hasan died fulfilling his wife's greed. He was happy just to love her and receive love back, so I am sure Allah will grant heaven for Hasan. He has lots of good qualities about him. He does not lie or cheat. He does not hurt other people's feelings. He worked hard to earn his food. He was simply a good human being who died fulfilling the wishes of his greedy wife. Hasan had done much good to other humans in spite of knowing there may not be any return of the favor, Hasan had a good heart. That is all Allah wants to see."

So the radiant angel said to Azrael, "I wonder if this human greed will ever end?"

Azrael said, "Thanks, Radiant angel. I will take his to soul to Allah now. Goodbye."

Wali Sahib noticed his five students were listening to every word of this story intently. They looked amazed at hearing such a wonderful story about the greed of the human race. Five of them had seen the story of respect. Now here was the story of greed. They were all wondering what the next learning lesson of Wali Sahib would be about.

Wali Sahib asked questions about his greed story, then requested answers from all five students, making sure they heard every word of that story. He was satisfied knowing all his students understood greed is not good.

When they had all finished eating their lunch it was rest time for his students in the afternoon. Wali Sahib went into his study room thinking it's time for me to talk to my angels now.

Unconditional Love

After dinner Wali Sahib asked all five students to join him for the lessons on love. He started by quoting some sayings and explaining how we humans come to understand them.

"Love knows no bounds."

He went on to tell his students the stories of Shirin and Farhad, Heer and Ranjha, Laila and Majnu, Romeo and Juliet.

"In all these love stories the young lovers die because they could not live without each other."

Wali continued, "Love is the most beautiful of all the feelings and emotions with which Allah has blessed mankind. These emotions, when experienced between two human beings who deeply and sincerely love each other, transform this world. Suddenly Earth seems like the most beautiful place to live in. Such feelings of love, when experienced, are so strong and powerful they create miracles."

Wali went further, defining the term unconditional love. "The best example is the way a mother loves her children unconditionally."

She goes through pregnancy, the labor pains of giving birth. The mother nurses her young and sacrifices her sleep at night to attend to her crying baby. She alters her day-to-day life to be there for her baby, to care for and love her child. This all happens because she has undying unconditional love for her baby.

"As the baby grows, this joy expands and becomes larger. The baby speaks its first words, takes its first steps. Soon months turn into years, until one day that little baby grows up to be a young man or a young woman. During this entire time, no matter how many hardships parents face, they always provide the best they can for their kids."

Wali said, in my opinion, the love of a mother for her kids is considered to be unconditional love."

Wali continued. "There are other kinds of love, too, love for your brother and sister, love for your relatives, love for your friends, and love for your pets. Love takes many shapes and forms in different peoples' lives. Some are passionate about their work, so their work becomes their love. I love to teach. I love to make clay pots. The list goes on.

As humans, our feelings may grow or fade with time. Kids love to play in a park, swing, and play with their parents or friends, whereas being adults, we don't enjoy the same things for ourselves, so young kids' love for things would be different than those of grownups. Adult love leads to marriage. How come that same couple goes through divorce?

There are several reasons two grownups eventually realize that their marriage is not working out. One of the main reasons usually is the love that had helped them to come together and make a decision of marriage has vanished, or at times love is still there, but love does not pay the living expenses. Hence, the wife leaves her husband or husband leaves his wife. Reasons are always there.

We humans have a tendency to rationalize things, justify our actions. For example, the husband left his wife because she could not give him any kids. After years of trying to have kids, he divorces his first wife to remarry a second one so they can have kids together. But love can take many shapes and forms.

The next day Wali looked all five students with him to show them an example of cruelty in love. A woman married a man who had a little two-year-old baby boy. Man's first wife had died from a cobra bite. The man, who could not work and take care of the young boy both at the same time, decided to marry another woman who gave birth to another son a year later. People always said this woman was the best step-mother ever, as she treated her step-son with more care and comfort then her own son.

Wali was taking his students toward this step-mother's home. As they were reaching her home, the woman stepped out of her home carrying her five-year-old step-son who could walk very well. He was enjoying a piggy back ride on his step-mother's back, an umbrella held over his head to protect him from the hot Indian summer sun. This was their routine to going to afternoon school. Her own son was walking bare-footed under scorching sun on the hot path covered with stones.

The students were a bit surprised, and wondered how this could be an example of cruelty in love?

Junaid gathered the courage to ask Wali Sahib, "How can this be an example of cruelty in Love?"

After the woman had walked a decent distance away where she could not hear Wali's conversation with his students, Wali replied to Junaid's question.

"This woman is showing care and providing comfort to her step son only. She gives him very good food, good toys, shoes, and clothes, but does not offer the same treatment toward her own son. She makes sure her son, who is learning from young age how to handle harshness of life, how to become rough and tough, how to manage with his belly only half-full. When these two boys grow up, her own biological son will already be prepared to face the harshness and struggles of life because he is learning this from a young age. Her step-son will face many difficulties and struggles, as he is getting used to a very good quality of life from this young age. She is setting her own son up for success, and her step-son for failure. So though everyone thinks she is a most loving, caring step-mother, I think she is the cruelest woman I have ever seen."

The following day Wali continued his teachings on the subject of love. When young people fall in love they surrender to their physical desires for each other and yet another expression of love blossoms There are many ways of describing these relationships. They may be called:

"Lovers"
"Love at first sight"
"I am falling in Love with her"

In some cases, because our human mind is far more superior then we realize, it is capable of loving the same sex. People who fall in love with same sex may be called gay or lesbian although Allah forbids it. And God, and most other religions forbid sexual relationship of same sex, too.

Wali went on to explain his understanding regarding same sex relations. Allah wants the human race to go on living. Marriage of opposite sexes allows a strong possibility the marriage will lead to offspring. Having sons and daughters assures that the human race will continue to exist. This is not a possibility in cases of gay sex or lesbian sex.

After breakfast the next morning, Wali gathered his students again and said, "Since my search from the beginning was for "Divine love for Allah," I didn't get entangled in worldly relations of various kinds of love, but kept my eyes and ears open and mouth shut most of the time and observed people around me intensely. A few years ago I had a very good student in my class called Kamaluddin. He liked being called Kamal, and was very honest about many things about his life.

He told me, "When I cannot hide anything from Allah who is responsible for taking care of my life, why should I hide it from anybody?"

So he shared a few poems with me after our lessons on love which I wrote down in my own book. It goes like this:

Afraid of Love, I am not. Afraid of Lust, yes I am.
Rarely do people understand the difference between love and lust.
They disguise Lust in the words of Love.
And relationships based on Lust can never last.

So marriage for all my students should be for pure and true love. When you are satisfied that the woman you are about to marry loves you just as much as you love her, then make that marriage commitment. Don't settle for compromises because only love will last. Compromises don't last.

Wali Sahib continues with a second poem which was a sad one.

Silence lives in the heart of the Lily
that grows in the darkest corner of my garden
It shivers in the cold night air and

tries to reach for the bright sunlight
but fails and falls down on the ground and gives away the soul.

Wali said, "This one is my favorite."

What is love.
Love happens by being together.
it only happens when two people are meant for each other.
Love is like a Rose that blooms on thorns.
Love is like a Ship that sails through stormy waters of sea.
Love is like a Road that leads to destiny.
Love is everything for those who understand.,
Love is nothing but a four-letter word for those who demand.
Love is true when you give, when you sacrifice
without expectations, without being asked.
This is what Love means to me, does it mean the same to you?
This is what I understand of love. Do you understand love as I do?

Wali noticed all his students were mesmerized by these beautiful poems.

He looked to see if his students understood the poem, and seemed as if they did. And Wali asked his students,

"Do you all understand, Love, Lust, and Compromise well?"

They replied, "Yes, Wali Sahib."

So he continued talking and said,

"Here is what I tell all my students: merely surviving on Allah's beautiful world is not life. Doing something meaningful and worthwhile is life. For example, most beggars who beg for food are usually homeless survive as do those who are poor and rich. Each survives in his or her own way. People who invent solutions benefiting the whole human race are remembered by name much after their death."

For example, in another part of our world far away from India is a country called Greece where lived a very wise man named Hippocrates. Hippocrates was considered the father of medicine. He performed the world's first successful chest surgery. In honor of his great teaching and practice as a physician, even today doctors take the Hippocratic oath. So his name lives on much after his death. He figured out how to benefit humans far beyond his village or country, and continues to benefit the world with his wisdom."

So, my students, don't settle for being an average merchant, an average farmer. Live beyond an average life. Use the wisdom I am sharing with you to create a better life for yourself. Reach out to as many people as you can and be a part of solution in their lives. Give as much as you can, knowing the more you give away with the goodness of your heart, Allah is looking at your heart, at all times he will give you more to give away. Allah has made this world beautiful and abundant. The land produces so much grain, fruits, source of all food comes from Allah's world if we humans learn to care and share, there is more than enough for everyone. As each one of us offers an oath to our creator, this world will become a most peaceful and much better world to live in than what we have made it into.

Wali then gave a homework assignment to all five students to read up on love stories from his library for next three days. Each student found a book and read for next three days. On the fourth, day Wali asked all his students about the book they'd read.

1. Javed had found a book about two young lovers. Sadly, their languages and cultures were different from each other's and both young lover's parents didn't want their children to marry each other. The girl's parents put conditions on her. Her mother said, "It is not love. It is lust, and if it is love, then you young lovers will have to prove it by staying separated for a period of 6 months. You are not to meet each other, not to talk, not even to write letters to each other. If at the end of the 6th month the two of you still have the same love that you seem to have at this moment, we will allow you to get married."

    But just when the 6th month was over and they were supposed to meet each other, the girl got raped by a young goon who attended same school as her. His sexual advances were ignored by the girl. Goon drew up a pornographic painting and showed it to the girl. Upon seeing the painting, the girl had slapped this goon. So the young woman gets raped by this goon and her lover is stabbed several places in his body by some local thief's. He is about to die when he meets his woman who is in lot of pain as well just after a rape. The author had done a good job of putting everything perfectly so the story had a tragic sad ending in which these lovers jump off the cliff to die together, saying, "If we can't live together we can certainly die together."

2. Junaid had chosen a story about a poor farmer and the daughter of rich parents, and how poor man does everything he promises the girl. Though fate has separated them, that same fate brings them back together. They marry, have children, and grow old together. The story ends with them dying in each other's arms.

3. Mujahid had read a book about a poor young man who chases his love to a big city where her rich parents had sent her to keep her from meeting him. The man does not give up. He goes to the big city, but all he knows is that his true love is here somewhere in this big city. After many struggles to find work to sustain himself, and after a few harsh years of rough city life, he finds his break in a stage acting career. He ends up becoming a successful stage actor and marries his true love. They live happily ever after.

4. Zahid had found a story about a poor family. The mother gets cancer. The father had died a long time ago. The son goes through many challenges and struggles to save his dying mother. Finally, he finds a doctor who manages to treat cancer properly. Hence, his mother is improving and her son is happy. Mother and son continue living happily ever after with each other.

5. Mazuddin found a very romantic novel where author described in vivid detail how both the young man and the woman went through many struggles and challenges in their lives. Even so, their love for each other grew with every passing day and, in the end, their love succeeded over all else. They lived happily ever after.

After his students had discussed each other's stories with Wali.

Wali said, "I hope I was able to teach all five of you something meaningful on the subject of love." They all agreed he had succeeded.

FOURTH WEEK

Lessons on Faith

This turned out to be a practical lesson. Wali Sahib went out to market, searching for someone able to catch cobras and other venomous snakes. He found a slim man who was known to help farmers remove snakes from the farm fields. People knew him as a snake handler, so Wali Sahib asked him to catch and bring a live cobra back to his Samajdar boarding school. The next morning the snake-handler came with a large black cobra eight feet long. Just looking at the big cobra frightened Wali's students. They immediately distanced themselves, wondering what Wali Sahib wanted to do with a cobra. He had the snake handler press the snake's poisonous fangs to remove the snake's venom. The handler squeezed the venom into clear glass. Because the snake was large, the snake handler was able to extract almost one quarter glass full of light yellowish looking slimy liquid. His task completed, the snake handler was paid and asked to release the snake where he had found it.

Next, Wali Sahib asked his servant to bring in five glasses of orange juice for his five students, along with one small table spoon. Breakfast was already over, so the servant returned with the five glasses of orange juice and a table spoon. His students were watching this activity their surprise growing by the moment. They knew Wali Sahib was starting this week with the lesson on faith, but they couldn't help but wonder what is going on. What did faith have to do with cobra venom? they wondered. Next, Wali Sahib added a spoon full of venom into each glass of orange juice, and asked his students to offer their prayers to Allah.

The students prayed silently for the next minute or so, then Wali Sahib asked all five students to drink the orange juice. Mazuddin's turn came first. His rational mind was screaming and questioning why Wali Sahib would want to kill him with cobra venom in his juice, but since he knew this week's lesson is on faith, he picked up the glass and raised it to his lips when Junaid shouted,

"Mazuddin, don't drink it. You saw our teacher put cobra venom into our juices. It would take only a drop of that big cobra's venom to kill anyone. A spoonful would kill you instantly."

Wali Sahib said to Junaid, "Shut up. Be quiet."

Junaid shut up right away. No one dared disobey Wali Sahib, especially his students. Mazuddin looked at Wali Sahib and asked Allah to help him. Closed his eyes and said, "BISMILLAH," and drank the whole glass of orange juice as quickly as he could. To his surprise, he was still standing moment after moment.

Mazuddin thought, "Since I am strong physically, it may take longer for the venom to work on me."

After a whole minute passed by he thought to himself, "Perhaps my faith in Allah and Wali Sahib as my teacher took away any effect of the venom on me. He knew he was experiencing a miracle of faith.

In his heart Mazuddin said, "Shukran Alhamdulillah."

The next student felt confident that if nothing had happened to Mazuddin, then nothing would happen to him either. He drank the orange juice and nothing happened. All four students drank juice with cobra venom and nothing was happening to them. Last was Junaid. He flat out refused to drink it thinking, because we are all young the venom is taking some time, but these stupid four students are surely going to die.

Nonetheless, Wali Sahib ordered Junaid to drink it out of respect for his teacher. He barely drank half a glass before falling down on the floor from the effect of the cobra venom. His orange juice also fell on the floor, the glass shattering into small pieces, orange juice spilling all over the floor.

Wali Sahib quickly sat down by Junaid, and moved his shirt aside and put his hand on Junaid's stomach. All four students could see yet another miracle unfolding. Junaid's skin was sweating, expelling, oozing the light yellow venom out of it. As each ounce of venom seeped out, Wali used his handkerchief to wipe it off. Junaid jumped up from the floor to stand on his feet and took a few steps away from Wali Sahib and the other four students, looking at all of them in complete amazement. Wali told Junaid, "Your education here is over. You may leave at once."

Junaid left immediately to return to his village. The other four students had witnessed a miracle unfold in front of their eyes.

Mazuddin asked Wali Sahib, "We are still a little bit shook up by our day's events. Why didn't the cobra venom kill us even though it was killing Junaid instantly?"

Wali Sahib replied, "What the four of you are experiencing and practicing is called faith, my students. Our human bodies are capable of doing things that seem impossible, but once you attach or add faith to it, the bodies can do things, that our rational brains are unable to understand.

"For example, I know of Islamic Shia Muslims who walk on burning coals on the tenth day of Muharram month. It is a time of mourning the death of Mohammad's grandson. The person who chooses to take this walk on burning coals does a Ghusl first, the full body Ablution required if the adult loses the state of body cleanliness. It is required before prayers and before all Islamic religious rituals. After Ghusl, the person does Wudu, then takes Alam in his hands, which can be heavy at times, before walking on a burning pit filled with fire. Shia Muslims practice self-flagellation and walk on fire prior to Ashura. Ashura is the tenth day of Muharram month.

"Just before they are ready to walk through the burning fire pit, hole made of burning coal their human body stays present, but their spiritual body takes complete control over them and they are able to walk bare-footed across the burning coals. The fire looks like a bed of roses to them. In fact, the bed of fire-burning coals gets so hot it is difficult even to stand five or more feet away from it because you can still feel the intense heat.

"I have witnessed this phenomenon with my own eyes. Our spiritual teachers call it mind over matter, demonstrating our human brains have powers beyond our own understanding.

"All four of you have utmost faith in your creator ALLAH, and me as your teacher, which is why the snake venom did not harm you one bit. Junaid was lacking that faith right from start. The lesson I showed him about respect where the goon almost killed him did not restore his faith in his creator or me as his teacher. That is why I asked him to leave my boarding school."

Mazuddin was paying very close attention to this lesson of faith because he had seen Wali Sahib perform the miracle that brought Junaid back to life from the effect of the cobra venom. Mazuddin quickly came to the conclusion in his head that faith can create miracles. The stronger the faith in your creator the more miraculous life becomes.

Lesson on Knowledge and Wisdom

The remaining four students gathered again after breakfast. Wali Sahib began by saying, "Knowledge is what one learns from life experiences. With the help of a good teacher, it can be learned from books in school. Knowledge about Allah is learned in a mosque, and God in church. Knowledge stays with us even when our worldly possessions are taken away.

"For example, knowledge of building a carriage occurs when the builder learns how to cut the wood and how to put it together. What started out as raw wood has been shaped and decorated and turned into a fine luxurious carriage. The art of transforming mere wood into a carriage is accomplished through knowledge. The same goes for an iron-smith. He turns raw, melting, hot iron into a sword or a dagger. A carpenter makes wooden furniture; a farmer has knowledge of farming. Some study medicine and human biology to become doctors, treating sick people and restoring them to health. The list goes on. This knowledge is yours. No one can take this away from you.

"We humans have to do something to earn our living, and we do what we can with our acquired knowledge. The carpenter cannot make a hundred chairs all alone, so he hires other people to help him get the work done. While helping new workers learn how to make furniture, those who are good learners, are responsible with their earnings, and have good business sense open their own furniture shops. They then hire new workers and the list goes on.

"This could be true in almost all trades. The one who makes the best-looking furniture that is also strong and reliable gets the best price and becomes rich. Some work on quality and some on quantity; again, to each their own.

"So knowledge helps human beings survive on this earth. Our human brain starts learning from infancy. Some things are instinctive such as a baby knowing how to suckle from its mother. From the age of one year onwards, human babies' brains start to recognize their parents' reactions.

A baby cries when it is hungry, and the parents feed it. It has learned that the next time it feels hungry and cries again, it will get fed. Sometimes, if the baby cries after drinking milk, parents then take the baby to a doctor to find out what is wrong. This learning goes on throughout our lives. The human brain is a most amazing organ that Allah created. It is so complex it is hard to understand it's abilities. This is where our knowledge is stored."

Wali said, "Here is a word - "IMPOSSIBLE," which actually means not possible. For example, we humans cannot fly like birds do or walk on water, hence, a person may say, "It is impossible to fly. It is impossible to walk on water, whereas some things considered impossible can be turned into "possible." Here is how "IMPOSSIBLE," word can be changed when you break it down. The same spelling becomes "I M POSSIBLE."

"A farmer knows how to farm his land, but my four students don't know anything about farming, so it is impossible for all of you to farm at this time. However, given training and actual practice, perhaps in two to three months all of you can learn the basics of farming, so the lesson on the word impossible is to know that Allah has given all of us exactly the same brain. What we do with this brain is up to us. If you apply yourself and put in sincere efforts and learn from your mistakes while you are in the learning process, making sure you don't repeat the same mistake again, you can do anything and everything. The more difficult the task, the longer the learning curve. This is why not everyone becomes a doctor or an engineer or a lawyer, but this does not mean one cannot become one, if one wishes to.

"I also wish to say to all of my students, 'Extraordinary people are ordinary people with extra ordinary determination.'

"IF you want your life to be extraordinary, you have to do something extra ordinary in your life. Failure is not when you fall down, it is when you don't get up again. It is better to teach a man how to catch a fish when he is hungry then to give him a fish when he is hungry. Today you will give, tomorrow who will give. Be self-reliant, don't be dependent. Self-discipline is best discipline.

Think positive, and your life will become positive.

Indian Folklore

There is a saying, 'A glass of water is half full or half empty.' Both are correct answers, but saying half full gives us hope, allowing us to look at the brighter side, and promoting positive thinking. 'Positive thinking will bring in positive results when applied in our day-to-day life. Being thankful to our creator at all times will make it easier to live in his planet Earth.

'A poor person was complaining to Allah I am so poor Allah my shoes are tearing up and I can't afford to buy new ones. As he was saying this to himself, he noticed a lame person who had lost his one leg due to an accident walking with the help of crutches. Instantly, the poor person got his reminder from Allah and said, 'Allah, I will never complain about shoes. I am thankful that I have two good working legs.' As the lame person saw the poor man jump over a puddle of water in his way, his instant thought was, 'Allah, why did you take one of my legs away? I will never be able to jump like that again.'

As he was thinking this, he came across a merchant's two sons whom he'd known since childhood. The merchant's younger son had lost both his legs to a tragic accident. He was being pushed in a handmade wheel chair by his older brother. Looking at this person in the wheel chair, lame man quickly got his reminder, 'Allah, my childhood friend cannot go anywhere without someone to push his wheel chair around. He cannot do many things needed in daily life. Someone has to put him in bed and take him to the toilet. He needs far more help than I do. Thank you Allah at least I have one good leg and I can use these crutches to get around on my own. Again, thank you Allah.

"After looking at his lame friend, the person sitting in the wheel chair thought, 'Allah has been unfair to me. He took both my legs away. I have become a burden on my family, I can't do much on my own."

As he was thinking this he also got his reminder and noticed a blind person holding a cane in his hands saying, "Can someone help me cross the road please?"

"The person without both his legs said to his brother, 'Can we please help the blind man first before going on our way?"

His brother agreed, and while helping the blind man cross the street, the person without both his legs asked the blind person, 'How long have you been blind?' And the blind person, who was used to people asking him all sorts of questions replied, 'Unfortunately, I was born blind. I still stay at my parents' home. They are very old and can't walk much now, so I am going to market to buy some food for our family. The blind person asked, 'Since you were kind enough to help me, a blind man, cross the street, may I ask you a question?' The brother in the wheel chair said, 'Sure. Go ahead.' The blind man asked, 'What is a rainbow?' and the person in wheel chair replied, 'It is very beautiful and pretty to look at. It is actually a bow or arc of prismatic colors appearing in heavens opposite the sun and caused by the refraction of the sun's rays in drops of rain. It has all the colors, and only appears in the clouds that have a lot of moisture in them, because it is sun light reflecting through drops of water in the clouds.

"Out of curiosity the person in the wheel chair asked, 'Why do you want to know about the rainbow?' The blind man replied, 'Every monsoon season my father encourages my mother to look at the beautiful rainbow in the sky. Though I have never asked my parents, I always wonder if this rainbow is the very most beautiful sight of all. Every monsoon season when my father sees it, he takes my mother out to show it to her as well. My misfortune is that I may never ever be able to see this beautiful rainbow in my lifetime.'

"By this time, the brother in a wheel chair was almost ready to cry and said to the blind man, 'In Heaven we will all be able to see better things than rainbows, and I have heard all blind people go to heaven.'

"In their talk they actually helped the blind person to the market, for which he was thankful. The brother in the wheel chair never complained to Allah about anything after this interaction with the blind. 'At least I can see Allah beautiful world. I can see the rainbow. Allah, I am thankful to you and will ever remain so."

Wali Sahib noticed all his students were paying careful attention to what he was saying and teaching. "So by remaining thankful and gracious to Allah, we look at the brighter side of life, thus promoting goodness in us and offers further hope, a will to survive and do the best we can with what is given to us by our Allah."

Wali then said, "Health is wealth, one cannot enjoy their wealth if they don't have health on their side."

Wali Sahib said, "Here is what I want all four of you to always remember. Money can buy the most comfortable bed to sleep on but it cannot buy sleep. For example, some people suffer from anxiety or feel their lives are stressful. Whatever the reason for the stress may be, they lie in comfortable bed but are unable to sleep. Many take herbs to help them sleep. A poor, worry-free farmer knows he is poor and doesn't have much, he has worked all day long. He eats an average dinner with his wife and kids, rolls out his matt on the hard floor and goes to sleep within minutes.

"Money can buy good food with excellent taste but cannot buy appetite. Due to health reasons, at times people are unable to eat what they wish to eat; at times we are simply not hungry. Here is an example. A farmer had just finished eating his regular ordinary lunch when a rich merchant who was celebrating his daughter's eighteenth birthday walked toward the farmer to offer him plate full of food. The food looked delicious. Even the smell of the food was good, but farmer who had just finished eating his lunch, had to refuse because there was no room left in his stomach, no appetite left.

"Money can buy you bodies with which to have sex, but cannot buy you true love."

Wali looked at his students to see if they understood everything. Convinced that they understood money is not everything and cannot buy everything, and that money can make life comfortable, but definitely cannot buy you happiness, he went on to the next teaching which was:

"IF money is lost, nothing is lost, as money can be re-earned.

"IF health is lost, something is lost. People cannot enjoy their own money without health on their side. Sometimes health comes back after treatment, sometimes it does not.

"IF a person's character is lost, everything is lost. A person should live to earn the respect of other people. A person's character speaks a lot about the person. One should honor his own word. Only say what you are able to do, and do everything good you are capable of doing. Let your actions in most cases speak louder than yours words.

"For example, a stone carver made a beautiful water fountain of an angel holding a water pot in Mazuddin's royal palace in Aurangabad. It was made so well out of marble that King Aurangzeb decided to keep it as welcome symbol outside his palace by the main entrance. He weighed the stone carver and matched the carver's weight in gold. Aurangzeb gave all that gold to the stone carver, and the stone carver's name and respect remains much after his own death through the art he created in his own life. One should not lie because when they are caught up in their lies they lose respect, and it is very difficult to live without respect."

Another example Wali used was, "Though a beautiful prostitute earns lot of money by taking off her clothes and pleasing men, these men do not respect this woman, so earning money is important, but earning respect should be far more important than just earning money. What you choose to do to earn your money can determine the level of respect you earn from those who know you. A good person who happens to be a good doctor is usually a well-respected citizen of his community."

Next Wali Sahib said, "Being a barber is fine. Just be the best barber in town. Love what you do, and do what you love to do for work."

He explained what he meant. "Being a barber is not considered the greatest thing to do trade-wise in India. However, being the best barber and loving what you do, helps you apply your best sincere efforts to excel at what you are doing. This comes from feeling passionate love for what you are doing. Obviously, as you get better and better at what you are doing, people who receive your services can't help but notice what the best work of being a best barber means.

No one is able to cut hair better than this barber; hence people line up outside his shop and pay his asking price for a haircut. At this point money becomes a by-product of the barber's love for cutting people's hair.

"Another example of excelling in what you do could be the carpenter who knows everything there is to know about his trade. People notice the fine craftsmanship and artistry in his work and pay him his asking price. Again, he is the best carpenter in town. The message is to be really good at whatever you do. Learn from the best. This world will always have people who use their brains better than someone else does.

"For example, people who use their brains creatively are often known as talented people. Talented people are good at problem-solving. They look for an upside in every situation and stay ahead of the crowd. These people become leaders, rich merchants, and business owners. Some of these talented people do not rest until they reach perfection in their line of work, knowing very well that only Allah is perfect.

"We humans can go only so far in anything we try to reach and achieve," said Wali Sahib. He instructed his students to surround themselves with talented people. "You will learn a lot from them."

The homework assignment was for each of his students to find a talented person, create an association with this person, and try to win the affection and care toward that student.

Wali Sahib explained, "Basically, I am asking you, my students, to create friendships with talented people."

Each student found a person skilled in their craft, and offered free services to become their apprentice.

1. Javed found out about a man who made the finest clay pots in town. He offered to help the potter at no charge, and learned a lot about pot-making and won the pot-maker as his friend.
2. Majahid made friends with a carpenter and learned the fine art of crafting beautiful furniture.
3. Zahid found a painting framer and developed the ability to frame great works of art.
4. Mazuddin found a talented ironsmith who taught him all about how to make weapons from raw iron, creating well-honed swords and daggers. He even made a beautiful peacock out of many small scraps of iron and hand-painted it very carefully. He gave it to Wali Sahib as a gift. It took Mazuddin a whole week to make this peacock out of metal and it looked amazingly beautiful. Wali Sahib was very touched by Mazuddin's thoughtfulness.

After breakfast Wali Sahib said to all his students, "Wisdom comes from learning from one's mistakes, being observant at all times and watching people do things that caused either success or failure. This is called learning from other people mistakes. Wisdom also comes from the ability to remember all these lessons I have taught you in these last five weeks, and implementing this knowledge to work around people. You can display wisdom to others and they will learn from you, my students. So wisdom is acquired knowledge put to work properly. This is what the saying 'older and wiser' means. It means the older we get the wiser we become because we are constantly learning lessons of life.

"Some people say Wali Sahib is a very wise man, full of wisdom. It is because I have devoted my own life to advancement in spirituality and so am able to benefit humans in many ways. This is how "Samajdar boarding school" came into existence."

Wali Sahib said, "All of you were sent to my school to become wise and become better human beings able to distinguish between right and wrong. Don't give in to temptations of wrong-doing because end result of any wrong-doing will eventually lead to disaster."

Wali Sahib said to his four students, "I hope I am able to teach all of you, how to become and remain good human being through-out your life."

They looked at Wali Sahib with utmost respect and appreciation in their eyes, and said, " Wali Sahib we feel blessed that our parents sent us to your school, we have leant so much from you, we will always remain thankful to you."

Mazuddin has been walking lonesome beach for quite some time now replaying past 5 weeks in his mind, and decided to return to Samajdar boarding school.

Mazuddin remembered clearly that he was most excited to go back home in a matter of a few days to tell his father all these great things he had learned. His own father had also told him about how to make his own life extraordinary.

He had said, "Do extraordinary things in your life."

And he thought how he had learned so much about making swords and objects out of metal. He had worked for the best iron smith in this village. He decided he would make his parents gifts from his new acquired skill of working with iron metal. It was his last day at Samajdar boarding school, when here came Azimuddin and shattered all his dreams of ever being a king. In fact, he was no longer a prince. He was Mazuddin, just Mazuddin.

Mazuddin had been walking on the lonesome beach for nearly an hour. Sunset was drawing near. He still could not stop the tears from flowing out of his eyes. He looked at the clear light blue sky. Knowing no one was around for miles in any direction on this lonesome beach, he said in very loud voice, "Why Allah? Why did you decide to turn my whole world upside down like this?"

And Mazuddin continued talking to Allah.

Knowing it seemed like a one-way conversation, this time he said, "Allah, I have been taught by my deceased father to dream no matter how hard or impossible or difficult, that dream might seem in a moment, because you would not give me the dream without also giving me the ability to make that dream come true. Today I am dreaming with my eyes open. I am making a commitment to you which I will keep at all cost. I will help as many people as I can in my lifetime. If that means helping the entire world, then so be it. I pray, you will grant me so much strength and wisdom that I shall not stop until such day I am able to make a positive difference in people's lives on a global scale."

By the time Mazuddin reached the Samajdar boarding school, the sun was almost setting. Mazuddin looked at the setting sun and thought. Sun, this morning when you came up at sunrise, I was a famous king's son, Prince Mazuddin. This evening as you go down in the ocean at sunset, I am nothing but just Mazuddin.

As Mazuddin walked inside the Samajdar boarding school he noticed Wali was anxiously waiting for his safe return and showed signs of relief upon seeing him.

"Dinner is ready, Mazuddin. I waited to eat dinner with you as all the other students have finished eating and are already in their bedrooms for the night."

Wali Sahib waited till Mazuddin finished eating his dinner before he said, "Mazuddin, I have spoken with three angels this evening asking if Bangkok, Thailand is the best option for you. All they told me is to send you inside the study all alone, and to close the door behind you."

"Mazuddin, I am not sure what their plans are. Are you willing to go into my study alone and take a chance with the angels? Anything can happen. The worst is you may end up dead. Many people experience heart-failure that leads to instant death when they try to interact with angels, so I am a bit nervous. Yet the angels, who usually answer either yes or no to my questions, did not make any comment on Azimuddin's idea about you going to Bangkok, Thailand."

Mazuddin was listening intently, and said, "I have nothing to lose and everything to gain. These angels are from Allah. They only harm people whose hearts are unclean. I know I am sure that have a clean heart. I am no longer a prince. My own parents whom I loved very much, are already dead, so if these angels decide to kill me then so be it. I will take my chances with the angels in your private study room with the door closed behind me."

Mazuddin's made his decision. He asked Wali Sahib when he was expected to go for his meeting with the angels. Wali Sahib, knowing very well a lot was riding on this meeting with the angels said, "Mazuddin, I am asking you to first take a shower, and recite some Arabic verses toward the end of your shower in the tradition called Ghusl. Follow it up with Wudu. Both Islamic traditions practice these cleansing rituals to keep the human body clean, especially before prayers. Please wear clean clothes after your shower."

Mazuddin finished his shower and sacred rituals, and dressed in half an hour. He chooses to wear comfortable Kurta Pajama Indian clothes.

Wali Sahib said, "Please take anything you value with you inside the room."

So Mazuddin took a hand drawn picture of his parents and his twenty-five gold coins which were in a silk cloth sack pouch. He put these things in his Kurta pocket. As he prepared to enter the study room, Wali Sahib stepped close to Mazuddin and gave him a warm big long hug and kissed his forehead.

Wali Sahib said, "You are the best student ever to attend my Samajdar boarding school."

As Mazuddin was entering the room and closing the door behind him, Wali Sahib was thinking. The angels didn't bother to tell me what their plans are for Mazuddin. These are Angels of Allah. First and foremost, they only follow Allah's orders. Whatever it is they wish to do with Mazuddin must be good, for Allah works in mysterious ways.

Wali Sahib decided to walk to his own room, and perhaps check on Mazuddin in the study room in an hour or so.

Mazuddin entered the dimly lit study room which had a nice big comfortable chair and a large desk in front of it. The left side of the room had shelves filled with many books written in the Arabic language. Since it was dark, Mazuddin could not see the color of this room, but by the way what little light there reflected on the walls, he guessed the color to be light blue. As he turned to close the door behind him, he started smelling something really good as if a thousand jasmine flowers were blooming all at the same time. Mazuddin felt a funny feeling in his back, a tingling. Never in his life had he experienced anything like this. Mazuddin was now closing the door behind him and thought to himself. Whatever it is, I am going to turn around and find out.

Turning, Mazuddin noticed three angels standing right next to each other, their clothes glowing in the dark. They wore long white dresses like people in Saudi Arab do. Their eyes shone light blue, and they were not standing on the ground they were floating in mid-air. Gravity did not seem to work on them. Mazuddin felt his heart beating faster as it did when he was swimming or running or exercising. He knew he was just standing there. What could be the reason for the faster heart-beat?

Perhaps seeing these angels was causing his heart to beat faster. He had never seen anything look as beautiful like these angels looked. Their glowing eyes were a bit frightful to look into, and within a few seconds Mazuddin realized he was unable to move his hands or legs. He just stood there like a statue. He thought perhaps the angels had hypnotized him.

Mazuddin stood there frozen like a statue. Though he had been there less than ten seconds, it seemed like an eternity. The angels came closer. They all touched Mazuddin on his forehead. A very warm feeling passed through his entire body and he passed out, fainting, then falling into a deep sleep.

Majid's father looked at him with deep love and affection in his eyes and asked, "Are you following my stories, my son?"

Majid replied, "Yes Abbu Ji, tell me what happened next to Mazuddin? Did he die?"

His father answered, "Mazuddin was transported back in time to a day before King Kansa launched his attack."

Aurangzeb asked, "My son, what are you doing here? You still have few more days in your last week to finish, before your education is done with Wali Sahib."

Mazuddin's last memory was his meeting with three angels. He quickly recovered from the shock of it all and understood the angels had sent him back in time to save his father and mother from king Kansa's attack.

Mazuddin asked his father to walk with him to their royal garden. He spoke thoughtfully while his father listened attentively, "Daddy, I want you to pay complete attention to what I am about to tell you. Please do not interrupt me before I finish."

Aurangzeb had never before seen his son look so serious. He answered, "Go on and tell me. I promise I won't say a word until you finish telling me what you wish to say."

Mazuddin carefully picked the words to express himself and said, "Father, a lot is about to happen tomorrow. I know this because Wali Sahib and Azimuddin know this for sure. In next few days you will be able to verify everything I am about to tell you. Please believe me and trust me on what I am about to tell you."

Aurangzeb looked confused and very concerned at the same time. He could not keep himself from saying, "Mazuddin my son, you are scaring me. What happens tomorrow? And how do you know what is about to happen tomorrow? Only Allah knows what is going to happen. We humans have no control over such things, and we cannot predict the future."

Mazuddin carefully explained, "Father, King Kansa is about to attack your kingdom, with the help of other three kings. They are joining their forces tomorrow at early sunrise. Unfortunately, you are recovering from malaria, and hence feeling weakness and fatigue. You are not prepared for a war, and will lose the battle in less than half an hour. There will be no chance for escape through the tunnel by the fountain where an angel is holding a water pot with her left hand. Pulling the right hand opens the door to a tunnel. This is our only means of escape. Daddy, I know all this because I had a meeting with three of Wali Sahib's angels. They sent me a few days back in time to save you and mommy along with Alamgir and his wife."

Aurangzeb could barely believe his ears, yet he had never said anything to his son about the water fountain statue of the angel holding a water pot with its left hand and pulling the opposite hand to open the tunnel door this information was 100% correct. How could Mazuddin know about his malaria? He'd just seen his son walk into the palace claiming all this information was true. The king decided he must speak with Azimuddin and Wali Sahib as soon as possible.

Aurangzeb said to his son, "This means we have absolutely no time to waste. Either I can prepare myself for a war or we must flee with our lives through the tunnel, then come back and deal with King Kansa once I have recovered from malaria."

Mazuddin said, "Daddy, I know I am young but I do think fleeing is a better idea, for now we can always get help from Amina the queen of Jhansi, and you can get Azimuddin to help you as well."

Aurangzeb said to Mazuddin, "Son, I agree with you. We should all flee for now and deal with King Kansa later on."

Aurangzeb got hold of his important soldiers and their families along with Alamgir and his wife Mumtaz, and asked Dilras to pack up enough food for an immediate journey for a week. Everyone met that afternoon at the fountain in the royal garden and left through the tunnel.

Their first stop was at the home of Azimuddin. Aurangzeb knocked on the door. Azimuddin opened it and stared as if he was looking at the ghost of Aurangzeb. Seeing Mazuddin standing right next to Aurangzeb gave Azimuddin a comforting feeling that somehow this was all real.

Azimuddin asked, "Please come in Aurangzeb. I am so happy to see you are alive. I am sure Wali Sahib pulled some miracle to make all this happen."

Aurangzeb, Alamgir and a few soldiers all went inside Azim's home, and after a quick glass of water and wash-up Aurangzeb said,

"Azim, my son Mazuddin says you gave him news of my death at Samajdar boarding school. My son says Wali Sahib arranged for his meeting with three angels the night you left to come attend to your sick wife, and these angels have transported Mazuddin back in time a few days to save me and others from vicious and cruel King Kansa."

Right away Aurangzeb added, "By the way, how is your wife? I hear she is sick, too."

Azim replied, "She is recovering very well. In fact, I managed to get hold of a very good doctor. Perhaps I can take you to him right away so you can recover from this damn malaria soon as well."

Azim sent his servant to fetch the doctor who had treated his wife's malaria, and this is when Azim and Aurangzeb sat down to discuss their next course of action. A trusted soldier was sent that same day to talk to Queen Amina at Jhansi. Azim sent his men to those strong and powerful kings who were very good friends with him. Everybody were given private rooms to spend the next few days with Azim.

Wali Sahib was called in, too. When Wali arrived, he was very pleased to see Mazuddin was still alive along with his parents, for his angels wouldn't tell Wali where Mazuddin had disappeared from his study room that night.

Wali Sahib said to Aurangzeb, "Allah does indeed work in mysterious ways."

Within the next three days, Aurangzeb had completely recovered from malaria, thanks to Azimuddin's skillful doctor. By the fourth day, Aurangzeb had the support of many kings, and Queen Amina's army. Hundreds of elephants and horses with over ten thousand marching soldiers were collected, and they all headed out toward Aurangabad, King Aurangzeb's kingdom. Everyone's wives, and even Mazuddin, were asked to stay back with Azim and his family while Aurangzeb left to get his kingdom back.

King Kansa arrived at Aurangabad the next day to find it empty, and no one guarding the main gate. He walked right in and knew somehow Aurangzeb had escaped with his family.

But how could he possibly know that I was about to attack his kingdom? King Kansa wondered. He knew Aurangzeb would come back to reclaim his kingdom. Knowing he had the army of three kings, he would be able to defeat Aurangzeb if he did decide to return.

It took Aurangzeb and his vast army only half a day to defeat King Kansa and his army.

Once the war was won, Aurangzeb had King Kansa imprisoned for life. While in prison, Kansa had repeatedly dreamed of slaying Aurangzeb's advisor and his wife, then Aurangzeb's wife in front of him, and then 5 days later Aurangzeb himself. Just when he was cutting off the head of Aurangzeb with his sword, King Kansa would suddenly wake up. The dream would seem real for a moment, but he always wondered. I am in prison. I know this dream is merely a dream, so why do I keep seeing this dream again and again? He also knew he would wonder about this dream for the of rest of his life in prison.

Aurangzeb thanked all Azim's friends, who were powerful kings themselves. He thanked Queen Amina of Jhansi and Azim and Wali Sahib. For a week, they all celebrated Aurangzeb's victory and getting his own kingdom back. Then they all went back to their respective lives.

Aurangzeb asked his beloved son to accompany him for a private dinner just for son and father. While at the dinner table Aurangzeb said to Mazuddin,

"My son, because your faith is complete, because you decided to take your chances with three angels, and risking your own life, I am able to have my family and my own kingdom. I am able to have this dinner with you. I will always remain thankful to you, my son."

Mazuddin then said, "Father, I am glad three angels decided to send me back in time a few days to help the whole situation. I remember walking on the lonesome beach outside of the Samajdar boarding school at sunset. Father, I had never ever felt such sadness and emptiness inside of me. In fact, I spoke to Allah and asked why he turned my world upside down like this. That same evening with the three angels, Allah decided to return to me everything any son could ever ask for, which is having a wise loving father like you and a mother whose love is limitless."

… and they all lived happily ever after."

Majid's father looked to see if Majid was paying attention or had fallen sleep, as he knew it was getting to be very late in the night. Nasiruddin noticed his son's eyes were looking very sleepy, but Majid was awake and still listening to every word of his father's story.

Majid's father looked at the big clock on the wall inside the intensive care unit. He could hardly believe his eyes. It was 2:30am. Nasiruddin said to Majid, "Son, I am very proud of you for keeping awake and listening to all these stories that I have been telling you these past eight hours or so. Now, do me one last favor."

Majid, who was obviously feeling quite sleepy, wondered what his father could possibly want from him at 2:30am at night.

So Majid said, "Abbu Ji, I am your son. I love you very much. You don't have to feel as if you are asking me for a favor. Just ask, Abbu Ji, and I will gladly do anything I can for you."

Nasiruddin then said, "Majid, never ever forget these stories I told you tonight. Promise me you will always remember them and someday tell them to your own son."

Majid promised his father he won't forget these stories. Since it was very late at night, he said to his father, "Abbu Ji, get some sleep. I will come late tomorrow morning to visit you again. I must go home now and get some sleep myself."

Majid gave his daddy a big hug and kissed him on his cheek. His father kissed him back and said, "I love you very much my son. Get home safely."

Then Majid said, "I love you too, Abbu Ji. Have a good night. Sweet dreams. I will see you tomorrow."

Majid started walking towards his home at late night streets were well lit, it was a short distance walk back to his home. Majid could not believe how much his father had talked so many interesting folklore stories, Wali's lessons on knowledge and wisdom beautiful poems in Wali's lessons on love.

While walking back home he recollected yet another interesting evening he had with his father when Majid was 16 years old. Majid's elder brother had brought home a movie called "Blue Lagoon." On a VHS video tape. Since the movie had some adult content in it Majid was required to watch this movie in supervision of his older brother who asked Majid to close his eyes as he fast forwarded this adult content. Majid found the lead actress Brook Shields of this movie to be his ideal visual picture of beauty. Majid had found a large poster of Brook Shields and put it on a wall in his bedroom.

This evening when Majid's father returned from his work and noticed a large poster of this beautiful blonde young girl with light color eyes, beautiful face features and blonde straight hair. He calmly asked Majid, "Son, who is this young beautiful woman in this poster?"

Majid replied, "Abbu Ji, this is Brook Shields from the movie Blue Lagoon."

Nasiruddin right away said to Majid, "Son, this movie had adult content, you were not allowed to watch this movie without adult supervision?"

Majid replied, "Abbu Ji, Sajjad my elder brother fast forwarded the adult content and asked me to close my eyes while he was forwarding through adult content scene."

Majid's father then asked, "Why this blonde woman's poster son?"

"Abbu Ji, I like her she looks exceedingly beautiful to me."

Nasiruddin then said, "Son, do you know she lives in America, and we live in India, she does not come to India and we don't go to America."

"Son, why don't you put a poster of Indian actress like Rekha, or Sarika at least I can take you to their home to have you meet them."

"Abbu Ji, you are contradicting yourself."

"Son, how am I contradicting myself? What do you mean?"

"Abbu Ji, you are the one who is teaching me telling me, son dream, no matter how hard, impossible or difficult, that dream may seem in the moment, Allah will not give you a dream without also giving you the ability to make that dream come true."

"So Abbu Ji, I am dreaming about living in same land as she, where I will be able to interact with women who have light eyes and blonde hair."

Nasiruddin asked Majid, "Please go bring me some medicine for thinning my blood for my heart condition, from our local chemist, my medicine just ran out yesterday."

Majid took the prescription and money that his father handed to him quickly put on his shoes and left to go get medicine for his daddy.

Nasiruddin looked at his wife Bilquis, who was present in the room while Nasiruddin was talking to her son about the beautiful blonde women's poster.

Nasiruddin then said to Bilquis, "Bilquis, your son Majid will do wonder for you someday, He sounded so confident about going to America, which is amazing for me."

"Bilquis I have been teaching him if you cannot encourage someone don't discourage them either."

"I don't want to tell him how far away America is from India, when it is day here it is night in America. America is completely on the other side of the globe from India."

"It takes two long flights to get to America. From India to Europe and from Europe to America."

"Not to mention it takes VISA in your passport to visit America, not everyone gets the VISA either."

Airline ticket to go to America alone can cost more money than some average people's earning in a whole year in India."

"Bilquis your son will definitely do wonders for our family someday."

Majid quickly shook him out of his thoughts as he had reached his home. He rang the doorbell. Majid's mother opened the door and right away said, "Majid it is so late at night what took you so long I was beginning to worry about you."

Majid said, "Abbu Ji won't stop talking to me, he pleaded me to hear his Folklore stories which are amazing Ammi Ji."

"Majid did you eat your dinner at all?"

"Yes Ammi Ji, daddy shared his dinner with me."

"Ammi Ji, I am very tied and sleepy I wish to wash up and go to bed at once."

Majid's mother went into the kitchen and brought him a glass of milk while Majid got done washing his feats and hands and face.

Bilquis said to Majid, "Please drink this glass of milk then go to bed."

When Majid finished drinking the Milk Bilquis took the empty glass out of Majid's hand leaned towards Majid and gave Majid a kiss on his cheek and said, "You are my good son, I love you very much Majid."

Majid kissed his mother back on her cheek and said, "I love you too Ammi Ji, I have to wake-up early to take breakfast for Abbu Ji in the morning now I must go to bed."

Bilquis said, "Sleep well my son, have a good night."

Next day early morning Majid woke up to phone ringing loudly by his bed he instantly picked up the phone and said, "Hello, who would you like to speak to?"

"This is Dr. Kulkarni calling, is Mrs. Nasiruddin available to talk?"

Majid called for his mother who was busy making breakfast for her husband in the kitchen.

"Mom daddy's doctor is on the phone asking for you."

Bilquis quickly came on the phone and said. "Doctor this is Bilquis, I am Nasiruddin wife, is everything okay?"

Doctor Kulkarni said, "I am sorry for the bad news Bilquis, your husband Nasiruddin passed away few minutes ago, you may come to the hospital to collect his dead body."

Bilquis put the phone down and Majid had never seen his mother looked so sad as tears were already rolling down her cheeks. She looked at Majid and said, "Majid your daddy passed away he died a few minutes ago."

Message

Message to ISIS and Sharia law imposer on non-Islamic people.

It is written in Quran, "Killing of one innocent person is like killing of all humanity."

It is also written, "An insignificant insect like ant, if you (Humans) can't bring it back to life, you don't have the right to kill it, giving life and taking life is in my (Allah's) power and department, let that remain my power and department."

Quran does not give permission for killing of another human being period.

Now what I wonder about is what kind of Quran members of ISIS are reading, are they following what Quran is teaching. They are giving Islamic people bad name around the globe.

Now I wish to address Shariya law Imposers.

North Europe, France, England, New Zealand, Australia, America. These were never an Islamic countries to begin with. No one begged Islamic Muslim people to come to these western countries. Muslims came on their own free will and to find a better way of life, to enrich their lives financially or whatever else might be the reason for your migration. These western countries have their own way of living their own lives. Western world people are not going to Islamic Muslim countries like Saudi Arabia and asking their Islamic Muslim women not to cover their bodies in Hijab (Burqa). Big black dress that cover's the bodies of women from their head down to their toe. So why does the Extremist Islamic Muslim people feel the need to impose Shariya laws on Non-Muslim Christian or whatever their religion may or may not be. France and England and other western world countries are their own homes.

They should be allowed to live however they choose to live in their own home countries. If Islamic Muslim people don't like the way western people live in their own homes, then they should leave their home countries and go back to Saudi Arabia or any other Islamic Muslim country where you will be allowed to practice your Sharia laws for yourself and impose it on others.

Allah looks at what is your Intention, what is in your heart, Allah is most merciful most forgiving most kind. Journey is written Allah know you from your birth to your death. Start point A to end point B. How you go about living from point A to point B goes with you to your grave, no one will come to help you in your grave only your deeds will go with you, your actions, your intentions behind those deeds and actions will go with you and you will be judged by Allah. To judge is Allah's department not humans. All Extremist Islamic Muslims should live by simple principals.

"SEE NO EVIL."

"HEAR NO EVIL."

"SPEAK NO EVIL."

"DO NO EVIL."

If you (Extremist Islamic Muslim's living in western world.) don't like the way western women dress up or dress less expose more. Or how they choose to live in their own home countries, ignore it or better still leave their counties and go back to where ever you or your ancestors came from. As we all know Islam did not originate in western world. Islam originated in Saudi Arab.

My sincere thanks to;

I wish to express my sincere gratitude to all of my readers for purchasing my book and taking the time to read it. I also wish to say thank you to Leonard Szymczak, for being my writing coach for helping with every step of book writing journey. I wish to say thank you to Joy Butler who helped me edit many chapters of my book. And I also wish to express my gratitude for CreateSpace website which has allowed a person like me for whom English is not their first language to help publish my book in English Language.

I also wish to sincerely thank many people who have been there for me at various stages and difficult times of my life in India and as well as in USA.

You guys know who you are, you also know who I am, and without your help I would have never been able to come this far in my own life. I thank you from the bottom of my heart.

I don't wish to list their names as they may or may not like it, besides this list would be very long.

I humbly remain thankful to you all.
Best wishes;
Majid.H.Nasiruddin.

95334442R00071

Made in the USA
San Bernardino, CA
15 November 2018